THE HISTORY OF
ROYAL AIR FORCE
COTTESMORE

GW00537747

NORMAN J ROBERSON & JACK G TALLISS

First Published in 1991
by GMS Enterprises
67 Pyhill Bretton
Peterborough
England
Tel (0733) 265123

ISBN 1 870384 09 1

Copyright: N J Roberson & J G Talliss

Body of text set in Times 9pt
on Apple Mackintosh DTP System

This title is sold in aid of the
Royal Air Force Benevolent Fund

Printed for GMS Enterprises by Nene Lithographic,
Nene House, Town Bridge, Peterborough.

FOREWORD

by
Air Chief Marshal Sir Neil Wheeler GCB CBE DSO DFC and Bar AFC FRAeS

One of the sad things for those of us who served in the Royal Air Force before World War II is that so few of the original flying stations still exist. Such names as Hawkinge, Tangmere, Netheravon and Hornchurch, for instance, are just memories. Another similar station was Worthy Down, my first station on leaving Cranwell. It was handed over to the Royal Navy in 1938 when the Admiralty assumed control of the Fleet Air Arm. Now it houses the Royal Army Pay Corps.

However, my squadron's departure from Worthy Down took us to one of the new RAF airfields being built at that time to very high standards, Cottesmore. I have now been invited by the Station Commander of Cottesmore to write a foreword to the history of the station. My only claim to fame is that I was adjutant of No 207 Squadron in 1938 and commanded the advance party of my squadron that arrived at Cottesmore on 20 April 1938.

Perhaps I could briefly describe what I found at Cottesmore. There was a fine grass airfield and it was obviously going to be a great improvement after Worthy Down, which was an airfield put on top of a 'down'. Before the war there were, of course, no runways military or civil anywhere in Britain. The station buildings, including all the messes and accommodation, consisted of wooden huts, but there was a great deal of building in progress. Nevertheless, until the outbreak of war we remained in wooden huts. The only permanent construction on my arrival were four magnificent C Type hangars, and each squadron acquired two. To us, after the World War I hangars at Worthy Down, they really were splendid with fine offices attached. The autumn air exercises of 1938 were the first time that the idea of dispersing aircraft around the airfield was introduced. We all maintained that servicing aircraft in the open would be impossible and, as soon as the exercises were over, saw to it that our aircraft were all safely (as we thought) tucked away in our great hangars! We were in for some surprises.

Before going to Cottesmore stories had reached us at Worthy Down that an airfield was not very welcome in the peaceful neighbourhood and renowned hunting county of Rutland, our smallest county. We were sympathetic and, apart from other considerations, did not want to leave Worthy Down. But we were determined to make a good start and, as soon as we had settled in, officers were selected to call formally on anybody of any influence in the neighbourhood. We also took particular care in handling any complaints about aircraft noise; and I am pleased to read in the history that this is still an important consideration on the Station. Needless to say we invited the Cottesmore Hunt to arrange a meet at our Officers Mess and my Squadron Commander, Squadron Leader J N D Anderson, hunted regularly. Looking back I can say with confidence that, when I finally left Cottesmore just before the outbreak of war in 1939, we lived happily amongst a most friendly and understanding community. I am, therefore, delighted to read that things have not changed.

During the past fifty or so years the Station has not only had a varied RAF life with many different roles but has been the home of Americans, Germans and Italians. It is, therefore, very pleasing to note that, in addition to the friendship of the local people, there has been, and still is, great comradeship between the RAF and Allied Air Forces at Cottesmore. Indeed, as the history relates, the USAAF left behind a bronze memorial plaque with the quotation 'May the memory of the comradeship sown in the skies of Europe forever be as green as the fields of Cottesmore'. Former USAAF members have taken a keen interest in this history and contributed to its completion.

I am particularly pleased that Cottesmore should now be the home of the Tri-National Tornado Training Establishment. As the Deputy Chief of Defence Staff (Operational Requirements) in 1968 I was intimately concerned with the requirement for a Multi Role Combat Aircraft, particularly the collaboration aspects, and later as Controller (Air) in the Procurement Executive 1973-1975 I was responsible for the British management of the three-nation team (German, Italian and British) that developed the Tornado. In addition I was also closely involved with the choice of name, which happily fits into all three languages.

I visited Cottesmore a year or two ago to give what assistance I could to the authors of this history, and was delighted that it was a Luftwaffe Officer who showed me around the Tornado. The general spirit on the station was a fine tribute to the whole concept of a tri-national establishment and fully bears out the great hopes expressed when the unit was first formed.

The authors of this book have made what might be a dull catalogue of units coming and going into a fascinating story of a very remarkable RAF station. I certainly learnt a lot from reading it. I am grateful for the pleasure it gave me and honoured to have been asked to write the foreword. For over 53 years, RAF Cottesmore has fully justified its motto: 'We rise to our obstacles'.

NEIL WHEELER

4

CHAPTER ONE

Wings over Rutland

"... how these curiosities would be quite forgott, did not such idle fellows as I putt them down."

John Aubrey 1626 - 1697

It was one of those dark, cheerless November days; grey veils of cloud swept low over the tree tops and the countryside looked its worst. Rooks were circling over the elm trees behind Cottesmore's village church of St. Nicholas when the crimson and yellow balloon was first seen drifting with the westerly wind. No one had seen anything like it before. Someone shouted to the pilot. He waved. People came out of their cottages; youngsters ran through the mud to follow it, farmers mounted their horses and set off in pursuit. A cold rain started to fall causing icicles to form on the pilot's clothing and forced the craft lower so that it barely cleared the pub at Greetham. A gust of wind lifted it up over the ridge and the Great North Road and finally it came to rest in the middle of Lord Lonsdale's hounds which were out hunting at Pickworth. The date was 1 November 1813, and Mr Sadler of Nottingham had flown 34 miles to complete the first recorded flight over Rutland.

The first conventionally winged aircraft to be seen in the area was probably Gustave Hamil's Bleriot which landed at Uppingham in 1912. Later, in May 1914 , Hamil flew over the North Sea and was never seen again. The Great Daily Mail 'Circuit of Britain' race also crossed the county in 1912 causing great excitement for the local people, many of whom rushed out early in the morning to catch a glimpse of the flimsy flying machines as they made for one of the turning points in the race near Melton Mowbray. One of the contestants, C P Pizey force landed in the Parish of Egleton in his Bristol biplane, but was able to continue after repairs.

Soon afterwards the countries of Europe were drawn into war. Soldiers marched to the battlefields in 1914 with the enthusiasm of the truly innocent, but soon, experience of the great static land battles on The Somme, at Paschendale and Verdun had disillusioned millions. While the armies confronted each other in the mud and desolation on the ground, in the air fragile flying machines restored the oldest form of war; single combat which attracted some of the brightest and most daring young men from all corners of Europe.

Away from the battlefields the civil population seemed to be oblivious to the realities of war although Cottesmore people were reminded of them from time to time, notably on the 3rd of September 1916 when villages in Rutland were bombed by a Zeppelin. An observer on a searchlight battery at Thistleton named Mr Beechcroft said that after the Zeppelin had bombed Nottingham, they were warned of its approach and could clearly see its lights and hear the drone of its engines before it dropped a stick of six to eight bombs between Sewstern and Thistleton, a few yards north of where Cottesmore runway is now situated. The Grantham Journal of the day carried a picture of the Zeppelin caught in the searchlights over Thistleton. As it flew towards the coast, the airship was attacked and shot down by Lieutenant William Leefe Robinson RFC of 39 Squadron.

When the Armistice was signed in 1918, the terms were such that the losing countries were subjected to huge reparations which could not be met. This led to the collapse of the D Mark. In 1914, for example, the Dollar had been worth just over 4 Marks, in 1920 it was worth 40 Marks, but by 1923 one Dollar bought 4,200,000,000,000 Marks as the Weimar Republic printed money to pay off the debt. Needless to say, leaders arose who were intent on restoring national pride and some measure of economic recovery, causing old aggressions to be re-kindled; and not without forebodings, re-armament began. The Luftwaffe was officially reborn in 1935. In Italy the armed forces were growing in size and efficiency. The Spanish Civil War in 1936 was the catalyst to an overt general re-armament in Europe. While the Luftwaffe in the guise of the Condor Legion and the Italian Aviatione Legionaria gave aid to General Franco's Nationalists, an international brigade of riflemen representing all shades of the left and central parties; trade unions, students, individualists and intellectuals fought with the Republicans.

With this European instability in mind the Air Ministry Aerodrome Board began to carry out air reconnaissance and to investigate a large number of possible airfield sites. A number were released for fully detailed engineering surveys. A Mr T Convey was tasked to survey one in Rutland which was to be referred to as THISTLETON to avoid any difficulties with the Cottesmore hunt. He was told to proceed with caution and keep a low profile in a rather 'sensitive' area. In order to comply with the letter of his instructions he took lodgings in a remote cottage with a farm labourer and his wife. However, it was not long before the local bush telegraph had picked up the vibrations and he received a call to take afternoon tea at the Cottesmore Vicarage where he was interrogated in the nicest possible way. 'I answered the questions as truthfully as possible' he said, 'and pointed out that the proposed airfield was listed as a fighter base which would of course defend Cottesmore village should the Luftwaffe decide to pay it a visit. This information circulated on the grape vine with the speed of light, and following a mass meeting of local people in the pub, I was asked to pass a message to the Air Ministry that the airfield had 'nought to do' with Thistleton; it was Cottesmore's own airfield and should be known as such. This information was of course included in my report with the survey and the name was changed to Cottesmore'. Construction of the airfield began in 1935.

The Royal Air Force at Cottesmore.

Cottesmore was the first of the three military airfields to be built in Rutland. Construction of Woolfox Lodge, three miles to the south east and North Luffenham, six miles to the south followed in 1940. Cottesmore is now the only one of the three still functioning as a flying station. It was officially opened on 11 March 1938 under the command of Wing Commander H V Drew OBE AFC.

On 20 April 1938 Flying Officer Neil Wheeler (later ACM Sir Neil Wheeler), Adjutant of 207 Squadron left Worthy Down in charge of some 300 airmen: armourers, fitters, cooks, batmen, clerks and all the other trades that made up the support personnel of a mobile squadron in those days. When they arrived at the newly opened RAF Cottesmore they found that the only two uniformed people on the station appeared to be the Station Commander, Wing Commander H V Drew and the Station Adjutant, Flight Lieutenant Whitlock. They saw four hangars and very little else save for a few small wooden huts and some tents used by the construction workers.

Like all the other airfields in the country at that time there were no hardened runways and they saw only a wind swept grass plateau standing 461 feet above sea level. Fortunately the underlying sandstone, marlstone and limestone rocks drained very easily and the wind helped to dry out wet surfaces quickly and avoid the quagmires that followed wet weather at many other airfields. 35 and 207 Squadron, each equipped with 12 aircraft, flew in shortly after the ground parties had arrived. 207 flew only Vickers Wellesleys, 35 also had Wellesleys and their first Fairey Battle, K7695, a dual control aircraft which they had received only six days before. Both types were a leap forward in technology over the Fairey Gordon biplanes

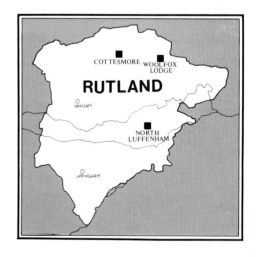

Vickers Wellesley K8530 of 35 Squadron at Worthy Down in 1938, just before the Squadron moved to Cottesmore. *(Photo: MoD)*

the squadrons had flown before July 1937. The two squadrons had a great variety of experiences and a certain amount of romance in their recent history. Both had been operating in the Middle East during the Abyssinian Crisis of 1935 living a 'Lawrence of Arabia' type existence. After disembarking at Port Sudan they had lived under canvas and spent the time patrolling railway lines from Haiya Junction to Kassala to Gederef; carrying out reconnaissance flights in search of suitable landing grounds, pioneering mail flights between Damer, Kassala and Khartoum, flying patrols along the Eritrean Frontier, and generally getting the wind in their hair and the sun on their faces.

After returning to the United Kingdom they received their first Wellesleys at Worthy Down in 1937, 35 in July and 207 in August. These new monoplanes had several novel systems including variable pitch airscrews, retractable under-carriages and flaps. The Wellesleys were not destined for a long career in the RAF but before they were retired they had at least one claim to fame. They broke the World's Long Distance Record for aircraft on 5th November 1938 when three Wellesleys, led by

Wellesley K7758 of 207 Squadron in 1938. *(Photo: P.H.T. Green Collection)*

Squadron Leader R Kellett, took off from Ismailia Egypt to fly the 7,162 miles to Darwin Australia. Two of the three reached Darwin on 7 November in just over 48 hours flying time, the third was forced to land at Kupang before crossing the Timor Sea. The aircraft's home base at that time was Upper Heyford and the SNCO selected to take charge of the ground party was FS Hearnden. His son, now WO Hearnden served at the Tri-National Tornado Unit at Cottesmore in 1988-89.

Apart from this epic flight, the Wellesley's career was short and undistinguished. Most of its problems were due to faults in the fuel system, where one wing drained before the other which sometimes resulted in fuel starvation to the engine.

35 and 207 Squadrons were re-equipped with Fairey Battles soon after their arrival at Cottesmore. The new aircraft were ferried direct from Ringway and the Wellesleys were flown to the Packing Depot at Sealand for transfer to the Middle East. The conversion of the pilots started immediately. There were no Pilots Notes in those days but there appeared to be no great difficulty in completing the conversion from the Wellesley, the main change being from the air cooled Pegasus to a liquid cooled engine: the Rolls-Royce Merlin. Squadron establishment was 12 aircraft, 11 Officers, 2 Warrant Officers, 18 Senior NCOs and included 6 airmen pilots and 115 airmen.

The international situation continued to deteriorate and the need to train new pilots became urgent. The only pilots with Permanent Commissions were the Squadron Commander and Adjutant who had been trained at Cranwell. In August 1938 Squadron Leader J N D Anderson took command of 207 Sqn from Squadron Leader J W Lissett. Flying Officer O'Brien Hoare's name features quite frequently in the Operations Record Book (ORB - F540) a demonstration pilot performing at Andover before the Imperial Defence College, at Old Sarum for the Higher Commanders Course of Officers and other venues. He almost lost an eye when a bird went through his windscreen, however he overcame the disability to become a night fighter pilot and eventually reached the rank of Wing Commander. He survived the war but went missing somewhere in the Gulf of Carpentaria during a violent tropical storm in 1947 delivering a Mosquito to New Zealand.

On 5 September 1938, a Limited Mobilisation was ordered and all leave was stopped, as Czechoslovakia came under threat. The democracies were however, not yet prepared to go to war to support a small country. Instead, the Prime Minister, Mr Chamberlain journeyed to Munich and returned waving a piece of paper, 'Peace in our time', and the world, with the horrors of a European War still fresh in the mind, rejoiced. There were only a few dissenting voices in the general euphoria, notably Winston Churchill's, who growled to an uncomfortable House of Commons: 'We have suffered a total and unmitigated defeat'.

In November, the squadrons increased their establishment to 16 aircraft, with 16 reserves for 35 Sqn and 5 for 207 Sqn. Some of the people of Rutland became convinced that there was no requirement for an airfield at Cottesmore, no need for noisy aircraft to fly over their quiet villages and squadron

Squadron Leader Chester, Officer Commanding 35 Squadron talks to the Cottesmore Hunt in 1939. *(Photo: J Dobson)*

35 Squadron aircrew in front of a Fairey Battle at Cottesmore in 1939. Sqn Ldr Chester, OC 35 Squadron is in the centre of the front row. *(Photo: Gp Capt W.A. Griffiths)*

officers thought it prudent to go out of their way to be considerate and civil to them. They called on prominent local citizens leaving their cards with invitations to the Officers' Mess, at that time a small wooden hut, and they extended an invitation to the Cottesmore Hunt to meet on the base - a tradition which continued for many years. Their good neighbour initiatives bore fruit and Sir Neil Wheeler looked back to that time as one of the friendliest between the service and local people that he remembers in his 41 years service in the RAF. The Officers' Mess was so small that several officers lived out in the local hotels. Mrs Anderson, the wife of the 207 Squadron Commander recalled that her husband lived out in the Crown Hotel in Oakham at the time.

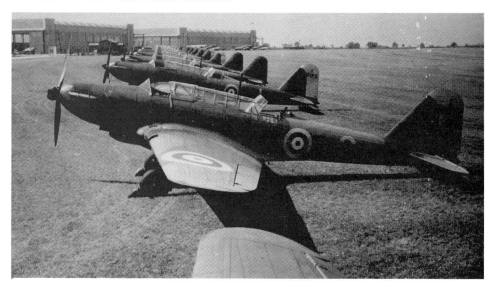

Fairey Battles of 35 Squadron at Cottesmore in 1939. *(Photo: ACM Sir Neil Wheeler).*

Three photographs of 207 Squadron's Fairey Battles in flight over Cottesmore during 1939. In the photograph right, note the grass airfield lying underneath the leading machine of the flight of five aircraft. *(Photo's: ACM Sir Neil Wheeler)*

L4962, a Battle of 207 Squadron at Spitalgate in 1939 *(Photo: R. V. Ashman)*

The Fairey Battle was powered by a single 1,030 hp Rolls-Royce Merlin engine. It was slightly noisier than the Wellesley, and had a top speed of 241 mph, considerably better than its biplane bomber predecessors but only marginally superior to the Wellesley. It was a clean looking monoplane with a glass house type canopy and a crew of three: pilot, navigator and wireless operator/air gunner. When it came to combat conditions however, its limitations were to be mercilessly exposed; it was too slow and too lightly armed to succeed against the battle proven and fast Messerschmitt Bf 109s.

The training of rear crew members was, compared to the pilots, unsystematic. As part of the Cranwell course all pilots trained in navigation and some specialised. In contrast, observers in the early days on the squadron were corporals although there were a few sergeants. Flying Officer Wheeler's observer, Corporal Patrick was an armourer by trade, 'a delightful man' who flew for six pence (2.5p) a day flying pay. The gunners were usually aircraftmen who flew as a part time activity from their primary trade.

By October 1938 Cottesmore had evolved into a training unit to provide crews for front line squadrons. 207 Squadron was ordered to exchange its Fairey Battles equipped with Merlin II engines, for the Merlin I equipped aircraft of 105 Squadron. Both 35 Squadron and 207 Squadron were training hard and trying out different tactics and techniques. On 9 September 1938 the unit diary reports 35

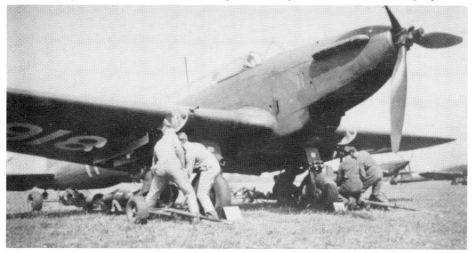

Bombing up K9180, a 35 Squadron Battle at the station for the first live bombing excercise on the Oakhampton Range during 1939. *(Photo: Gp Capt W A Griffiths)*

11

Squadron flying long distance formation and cross country flights of 6 hours duration covering some 900 miles. Much of the training was carried out at medium level, around 10,000 feet. That this was a dangerous height to fly, was tragically proved later in France. When some low-level formation was tried, 35 Squadron aircraft became over enthusiastic and flew low over the Oakham show provoking letters of protest.

207 Squadron carried out experiments at night with an angle of glide indicator at Otmoor Range near Oxford and practised high-level and low-level bombing. Training at night became more intensive as the winter months approached and on 13th December 1938 during a night exercise 207 Squadron lost one of their most experienced crews when Pilot Officer P C Rolls who had been with the squadron since 24 April 1937 struck a tree 1,000 yards short of the airfield. On 23 March 1939, also during night flying, Pilot Officer G C Shepherd, his observer, Sgt. F C T Norman and the wireless operator AC1 J T S Randle were killed when their Fairey Battle crashed at Mileham near Swaffham.

Two views showing the airfield and it's aircraft.
Above: 35 Squadron (front row) and 207 Squadron with hangars in the background *(Photo: ACM Sir Neil Wheeler.) Below:* A similar line up. *(Photo F.W.S. Keighley)*

Spring 1939 saw an increase in international tension. Leave was again cancelled and the squadrons stood by for a move to a dispersal airfield. The feeling of disbelief among the Cottesmore personnel that war was a serious possibility gradually melted away as they saw signs of preparation all around them. Buildings were camouflaged, nets placed over hangars, pillboxes constructed, air raid shelters dug, the white aircraft serial numbers and the yellow edges on the roundels of the aircraft painted out and identity discs were issued.

On 1 May 1939, Wing Commander E B Grenfell AFC (promoted to Group Captain on 1 July), assumed command of the Station and the squadron establishments were again increased, this time to 24 aircraft each with 8 in reserve. On 13 May 35 Squadron was affiliated with 15 and 40 squadrons to provide them with manpower in the event of losses, and in June, three of their aircraft and crews joined 15 Squadron. This was the beginning of a continuing process.

Fg Offs Sandy Lane, Bingham Hall and Neil Wheeler in a Fairey Battle at Cottesmore during 1939
(Photo: ACM Sir Neil Wheeler)

On 12 July 1939 35 Squadron received two Ansons to help with the training of observers, wireless operators and air gunners. At the same time 207 Squadron flew to Evanton, Ross and Cromarty in Scotland, for one months intensive training for their observers, wireless operators and air gunners, and came to be regarded as a specialist unit for this work. Then on 24 and 25 August 1939 both squadrons left Cottesmore for Cranfield to serve as reserve units to cover war losses. They were not kept waiting long.

Nine days later all ten squadrons of Fairey Battles from 1 Group, comprising 12, 15, 40, 88, 103, 105, 142, 150, 218 and 226 squadrons (a total of 160 aircraft), the Advanced Air Striking Force (AASF), slipped out of England for grass airfields near Rheims in France. The next day, 3 September 1939, war with Germany was officially declared.

War is declared...

As soon as the Battles had landed they were made ready for action, to begin reconnaissance operations almost immediately. The first air to air combat took place on 20 September when three 88 Squadron

Handley Page Hampden L4194 of 185 Squadron pre-war. *(Photo:MoD)*

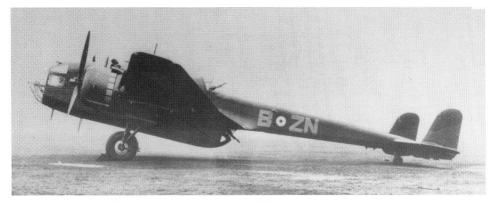

A 106 Squadron Hampden. *(Photo: via P.H.T. Green)*

Battles from Mourmelon-le-Grand were attacked by Messerschmitt Bf109s. Two of the Battles were quickly shot down in the first pass by the fighters, but the gunner of the third aircraft, K9243, Sgt. F Letchford, returned their fire and shot a Messerschmitt down; the first recorded German aircraft of the war to be shot down by the RAF. Ten days later 5 Battles from 105 Squadron at Ecury-sur-Coole were attacked by 15 Messerschmitt Bf109s. Only one Battle survived, and that riddled with bullets. It quickly became clear that they were no match for the day fighters and it was decided to withdraw them immediately from daylight sorties.

When Von Bock's assault smashed across the River Meuse in the early light of 10 May 1940 to end the so called 'phoney' war, 100 Fairey Battles were serviceable and ready. Thirty two of them took-off to attack German ground forces advancing through Luxembourg; 13 were shot down by the fearsome flak. More were lost in a similar attack later the same day. The following day a further eight Battles attacked and only one returned to base. Although they were outclassed by the fighters and slow enough to be easily picked off by the flak, there were many examples of extreme gallantry by these crews. One such followed the appeal from the Belgian authorities for help, to stem the flow of advancing infantry who had captured several bridges across the Albert Canal. Five volunteer crews from 12 Squadron operating from Amifontaine, took off on 12 May to attack two of these bridges, at Vroenhoven and Veldwezelt. Not one returned. The first two failed to reach the target. The second

Another 106 Squadron Hampden, this time seen at Cranwell pre-war.
(Photo J Hancock via P.H.T.Green)

14

Cottesmore's Officers Mess during the winter of 1939 *(Photo F.W.S. Keighley)*

formation of three were led by Flying Officer D Garland in P2204 who came in low through a hail of flak to score a direct hit on the bridge at the same moment that his aircraft was hit by ground fire and destroyed. The next two aircraft were hit and set on fire before they could release their bombs; one of the crews survived to become prisoners of war; the other crew did not. Because it was their bomb which hit the bridge, Garland and his navigator Sgt. T Gray were awarded posthumous VCs, the first to be awarded to an RAF crew in the war. The gunner, LAC Reynolds received no award.

At the end of that day 62% of all the Fairey Battles that had taken off had failed to return. On 14 May the entire surviving force of 62 Battles got airborne to attack pontoon bridges near Sedan - 35 of them failed to return, by far the highest casualty rate ever experienced by the RAF. The remaining Battles continued harassing attacks on the advancing forces, communications, airfields and targets of opportunity suffering further losses. The blitzkrieg rolled on with a relentless, unstoppable momentum. Flying in the teeth of the barrage from the 88mm guns, small arms fire and the ever present Messerschmitts, the Battle crews faced a nightmarish ordeal. By 15 June 1940 they had lost the equivalent strength of their entire force on the first day of the attack. Later that day, the exhausted, dispirited remnants were ordered to return to England.

So ended the short and bloody career of the Fairey Battle at Cottesmore and afterwards in France. Flight Lieutenant Wheeler was one of the few to survive his tour on Fairey Battles in 1940. He converted onto Spitfires, a very different proposition, and spent the next few years flying unarmed photo reconnaissance versions of the aircraft. From the time of Dunkirk large numbers of Spitfire fighters were reaching the squadrons and so the scene was set for one of the classic duels of aviation history: the Spitfire versus the Messerschmitt.

1939-1940 - the Hampden arrives!.

The Fairey Battles departing Cottesmore were replaced by 106 and 185 squadrons from Thornaby, Yorkshire. Both squadrons had been formed at Abingdon, Oxfordshire, during the general re-armament programme in 1938. Three months later they were re-equipped with the newer Fairey Battle. In October 1938 they moved to Thornaby where a very short time later they received the new Handley Page Hampdens.

The Hampden was named after a small Buckinghamshire village but was known generally as the 'Flying Panhandle.' With the Wellington and Whitley bombers it formed the spearhead of the RAFs heavy bomber force until the four engined heavies became available in 1942. The Hampden was powered by two Bristol Pegasus 1,000 hp radial engines with variable pitch airscrews and had several advanced features for its time. Its tapered wings incorporated Handley Page slots on the leading edge and flaps on the trailing edge which permitted a low landing speed of 73 mph with a very respectable top speed of 265 mph.

The first 185 Squadron Hampden touched down at Cottesmore on 24 August 1939. One by one the others appeared over the airfield, did a careful circuit to make sure that they had identified the correct field and landed. This care was necessary as the navigation aids at this time were rudimentary. Although the main emphasis being placed on good instrument flying and the use of visual pin points, it was by no means unusual for aircraft to become lost, especially in bad weather. 106 Squadron, also equipped with Hampdens, followed on 1 September, two days before war was declared.

The two Squadron Commanders, Wing Commander E D Barnes AFC of 185 Squadron and Squadron Leader W C Sheen of 106 immediately put their crews on an intensive period of training. They had found that the Hampden needed very careful watching; it tended to swing violently on take off and had an unfortunate habit of dropping a wing if the engine stopped on that side. An experienced pilot could counter this if he acted quickly; an inexperienced pilot, particularly if flying in cloud or at night could allow the aircraft to slip into a spiral dive from which there was no recovery. One of the greatest of all bomber pilots, Guy Gibson was well aware of its shortcomings. He recorded his own breezy impressions as he went out to check his aircraft at Scampton a few minutes after hearing that war had been declared:

'I went out to look over Hampden C Charlie and found her sitting in her usual dispersal point. She was my own aeroplane, and a lousy one at that. On take-off she swung like hell to the right and flew into the air with her left wing low. Sometimes an engine died out, but that was nothing - we loved her because she was ours'. (Enemy Coast Ahead. Guy Gibson, Pub Michael Joseph Ltd 1946.)

However, losing an engine on a Hampden for a less experienced pilot usually had far more serious repercussions.

With the reorganisation of the Bomber Command Groups at the beginning of the war Cottesmore became part of 5 Group. The squadrons lost their front line status to become reserves to cover war wastage and to provide trained crews for the front line squadrons. To avoid surprise Luftwaffe attacks on the airfield the squadrons dispersed to Evanton, and Kidlington in Oxfordshire; needlessly as it happened, because the Luftwaffe (and the RAF) were restricted to maritime targets at this time. It was not until the blitz on Rotterdam in May 1940 that all restraints were abandoned, and both Squadrons returned to Cottesmore.

106 Squadron departed for good to Finningley near Doncaster on 6 October 1939. 185 Squadron remained to train Hampden crews for the main force and as such became part of 6 Group, Bomber Command's training group.

This was a time of rapid growth in the size of Bomber Command; the capabilities of the newer, heavier aircraft were being tested for the first time and many were found wanting: radios, navigation aids and self-defence equipment all left much to be desired. This led to modifications, changes in tactics and the introduction of some variants. One of these was the Hereford which was identical in every respect to the Hampden, including performance, apart from its 1,000 hp Napier Dagger in-line engines which replaced the Pegasus radials. 185 Squadron had the misfortune to be equipped with a small number of these. One of its three flights had received Hereford L6005, just before leaving Thornaby, in Yorkshire, for Cottesmore, receiving two more during September, the flight receiving its sixth and last one, L6016, on 10 January 1940. Its arrival at Cottesmore was inauspicious. On 28 October Hereford L6007 made a perfect approach to the airfield and crashed on landing when the undercarriage collapsed. It was then used as a ground instructional airframe. This was the first of many Hereford incidents, mostly concerning engines which had a tendency to overheat especially when taxying. Various remedies were tried to cure the problem including adding cooling gills to the rear of the cowling, but these vibrated to the closed position and could not be re-opened in flight. Only one

Herefords of 14 OTU during 1940. *(Photo: 'The Aeroplane').*

operational mission was flown by a Hereford during the war, that being with 185 Squadron, and apart from their use at Cottesmore where they spent most of their time unserviceable, the majority languished away the early part of the war at Upper Heyford with No 16 Operational Training Unit (OTU). Only 150 were built, twenty three of them later being converted to Hampdens.

The Hampdens (and Herefords) carried a crew of four. The pilot sat alone in a fighter like cockpit with a single fixed Browning gun on his port side. The navigator sat below and behind the pilot and moved forward to the perspex nose for bombing. The other two crew members were a wireless operator/air gunner and a gunner; each equipped with a single (later a pair) of Vickers K .303 machine guns, one in a dorsal mounting, the other in a ventral position, both firing rearwards. Unfortunately, these guns had a limited movement in the horizontal plane. The operational Hampdens were thus extremely vulnerable to the Messerschmitt Bf109 and Bf110 crews who very quickly discovered this weakness. The 109s either attacked from the beam or silenced the gunners from long range with their canons before closing to finish the operation. The 110s evolved their own unique method. Their main armament fired ahead but they had one gun which could be fired sideways. They simply flew in formation with the Hampdens about 50 yards away and slightly in front and leisurely shot them to pieces!.

The Hampden crews were subject to other discomforts; they had very cramped crew accommodation, the ventral gunner in particular was so tightly wedged that there was no room for a parachute. And then there was the cold. The winter of 1939/40 was a notoriously bitter one, not only at Cottesmore but all over Europe with heavy snow falls and freezing temperatures for months. At altitude the gunners' fingers became literally frozen stiff so that they were sometimes unable to fire the guns when they were attacked. Perhaps the cold was the thing above all others that the crews remembered about the aircraft.

All three of the RAF's 'heavy' bombers, the Wellington, the Whitley and the Hampden and also the Blenheim medium bombers, received such a mauling at the hands of the Luftwaffe day fighters with negligible results to show for the loss of aircrew, that they were withdrawn from daytime ops in December 1939.

As a result of this decision, an important part of the training at Cottesmore became navigation exercises by night. The bombers now had to find their targets on dark and dirty nights, sometimes above cloud with very few navigation aids. Dead reckoning by day with the help of the odd pin point and accurate flying by the pilot was one thing, at night it was quite another. On a clear night, astro navigation was a possibility if the aircraft had a suitable place to hang the sextant and if the pilot could hold the aircraft steady for a minute or a two minute shot and if the navigator was skilled enough to identify the correct star through a canopy of varying transparency and could work out intricate calculations and apply numerous corrections to allow for the rotation of the earth on the bubble in the sextant; this in the cold and vibration of an aircraft. Even without the intervention of enemy action this was no mean task. Blind navigation therefore tended to depend more on loop bearings from beacons in the United Kingdom obtained by the wireless operator from a radio that frequently crackled with interference. The beacons were subject to moves to code positions, and of course, the further away from the transmitter the aircraft was, the less accurate the bearing became. It was far from easy but experience, skill, determination and luck helped. The Cottesmore crews worked at it and gradually became more proficient.

As the New Year turned to Spring, large numbers of aircrew began to arrive at Cottesmore. It soon became obvious that the reserve squadron system was inadequate for the task and so they gave way to large OTUs. In the re-organisation 185 lost its squadron status on 8 April 1940 and became 14 OTU with an establishment of 32 Hampdens, 24 Ansons and later 16 Herefords. A new 185 Squadron was immediately reformed, but it was only in existence for a further 6 weeks before it was finally disbanded on 17 May, with all its aircraft and aircrew being absorbed into 14 OTU. Group Captain F H Laurence MC assumed command of the Station on 21 May. Until 1942 the front line bomber crews had to learn the finer points of bomber operations by trial and error over enemy territory. They frequently flew their own routes, took off at a time to suit themselves, chose their own altitude to fly and were sometimes given a choice of targets. Some crews preferred to gain as much height as possible, some pilots, like Gibson, liked to go in low, he also developed a dive bombing technique that was hair raising for his crew and grossly fatiguing for his Hampden which he named 'Admiral Foo Bang.' After he had well and truly hammered it on a series of sorties in which he had thrown it around like a fighter and subjected it to stresses that the designer had never envisaged, it was donated to 14 OTU as a training aircraft. The practice of passing on well used squadron specimens to OTUs was common and may well have contributed to the very high accident rates there. Of fifty-three crashes of Hampdens and Herefords flying from the three Rutland airfields, recorded between 28 October 1939 and November 1942, almost all were training accidents.

The Luftwaffe was also learning painfully. They too began with attacks on shipping, then after Dunkirk the attacks switched to the fighter airfields on 10 July 1940 at the beginning of the Battle of Britain. Their bombers found what the RAF bombers had found; that daylight attacks against targets defended by determined fighters was a costly business. Although they had the advantage of fighter escorts, the result was the same with steadily mounting losses until the climax of the battle on 15 September when the fighters claimed 185 successes during the day (later more objective analysis put it at 60).

The Luftwaffe attacks...
Cottesmore was first attacked on 26 June 1940. A single bomber dropped a stick of bombs across the airfield. Most fell harmlessly, but four of the Officers' married quarters were slightly damaged. There were no casualties among the aircrew who were occupying them at the time. The attack alerted the authorities to the possibilities of decoy sites away from the main airfields. Q sites were lit to resemble operational airfields at night. K sites were more elaborate affairs to fool the daylight bombers with dummy aircraft, buildings and revetements. Decoy sites were built at Swayfield, 5 miles north east of the airfield on Honeypot Lane; at Pickworth and at Swinstead near Grimthorpe Castle, the grandest house in Lincolnshire. Swayfield was successful in attracting two attacks in May 1941. On 4 May an enemy bomber dropped five bombs and on 12 May two aircraft dropped six from about 8,000 feet. They were engaged by anti-aircraft fire from the site but without success.

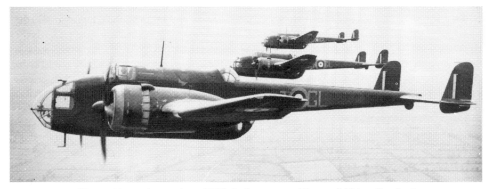

Three Hampdens of 14 OTU during 1940 *(Photo: IWM collection)*

Perhaps it was the first attack on Cottesmore that suggested a way of hitting back in a modest way at negligible cost to themselves. There was still (at this stage) a concern that the RAF should not attack civilians. The Government had issued 'Revised Instructions' to the Air Ministry in June 1940 insisting that 'the attacks must be made with reasonable care to avoid undue loss of civil life in the vicinity of the target'. If they could not hit the target they were told to bring the bombs back. Later came the concept of 'last resort' targets. Self evident military objectives (SEMOs) were authorised if the primary target could not be located. For some time the Whitleys of 4 Group had been dropping leaflets over Germany. This may seem to have been a poor response to bombing. They did show one thing however and that was the contrast in losses between their operations at night and the heavy losses sustained in daytime. They found that the training in navigation and night flying over enemy territory was invaluable and they were also able to report back on such things as airfields, defences, blackouts in the towns, position of searchlights, beacons and the like. Sir Arthur Harris who would take over Bomber Command in 1942 snorted 'that they had done no more than provide the enemy with five years supply of lavatory paper'. Be that as it may, on 25 July 1940, a few weeks after the evacuation of the BEF from Dunkirk three Hampden aircraft from 14 OTU took to the air on the first of many 'Nickel' raids, as they were called, over Northern France. As well as the bundles of leaflets each aircraft carried two 250 pound bombs.

The Station Commander briefed the three crews in front of a map of Europe. He told them that this was Cottesmore's first opportunity to blood its crews in action. They would fly over Northern France and in addition to dropping leaflets they would drop their bombs on any airfield that could clearly be identified as such. They were to keep their eyes open and bring back any intelligence of value. Four more Hampdens flew on other 'Nickels' on the nights of 13 and 16 August. All these raids were uneventful and all aircraft returned safely.

As the Luftwaffe assault on the fighter airfields developed, several raiders penetrated further inland. On 26 August, wailing sirens announced the arrival of another intruder overhead Cottesmore. It was a clear day and the German bomb aimer could see the aircraft parked on the dispersals. His stick of bombs fell near enough to damage three of the Hampdens. Further attacks came on the 6th and 9th of September and again on the 13th when four high explosive (HE) bombs in the vicinity of the Officers' Mess caused some damage to buildings and injured two airmen.

Cottesmore's war seemed to be hotting up. The 'Nickels' continued and on the night of 10 September Flight Lieutenant Deane, Flying Officer Smales and Sergeants Bazely and Coney in Hampden L4308 were briefed to release their bundles over Lille, Pilot Officer Evans, Pilot Officer Grant, Sergeants Farquhar and McCullum in Hampden L4204 over Amiens and Sgts Welch, Bowden, Brown and Sheen over Rouen. The first crew was driven to the aircraft as the dusk settled over the

19

airfield. It was a warm and hazy night and smoke could be seen rising from burning stubble in some of the neighbouring fields, as the flames were beaten out before the blackout started. Flight Lieutenant Deane heaved himself up into the pilot's seat and the others squeezed themselves into their crew positions sweating a little in their heavy flying jackets. One of the ground crew helped the pilot into his safety harness. Deane nodded his thanks. At a signal from the marshaller he started an engine, then the other. After running them up for a few moments he taxied out past the caravan and turned into wind. The Hampden was heavier than usual with the two 250 pound bombs and he wasn't sure how it would handle. An Aldis light flashed from the caravan and he opened both throttles to full power and flicked off the brakes. The Hampden lumbered forward and as the tail slowly lifted he caught the swing with a touch of rudder. He eased it off the ground by working the tail trimming tabs and didn't see the trail of dust he had left behind over the airfield. They did not see the French coast, nor were they sure that they were over Lille on ETA but they released the leaflets. They looked carefully for airfields but saw none and so they brought their bombs back as briefed.

Pilot Officer Evans' crew saw very little either, but they released their leaflets on ETA for Amiens and brought their bombs back. As they came up to ETA UK coast, Evans throttled back and settled into a slow descent hoping to pick up a recognisable feature. They had been without a reliable fix for over three hours. They saw nothing. Fifteen minutes went by, then another ten. Evans called Cottesmore for a homing bearing. To his relief they replied and continued with a series of bearings until he was able to pinpoint himself just to the west of Peterborough. A pale glow was in the east behind him as he went through his landing checks: brakes, undercarriage, flaps. He felt the thud as the undercarriage locked down, he glanced at the two green lights for confirmation and then concentrated on his approach. He touched down on the welcoming grass at 0610.

The third crew, Sgt. Welch's, positively identified Rouen; they also saw a flare path through a gap in the clouds and dropped a bomb on it. Why only one was not mentioned in the report. It is possible that the other hung up as other incidents of this nature frequently occurred during the 'Nickels'.

The next night, 11 September, Flying Officer Foster and Sergeants Tiley, Williams and Johnson had just taken off from Cottesmore when they were attacked by an enemy aircraft. The port engine was hit and stopped and the three rear crew members were injured, Williams seriously. Foster fought with the heavy aircraft trying to hold the wings level until he could get into a position to put it down on the airfield. He almost succeeded but just before touchdown it started to slip into the dead engine, however he landed the aircraft well enough to save his crew although the aircraft was seriously damaged.

On 26 September the recently promoted Flight Lieutenant Guy Gibson, wearing his new DFC ribbon, left 83 Squadron at Scampton and with other experienced bomber operators; Withers, Murray, Lewis, Pinchbeck, Smith and Redpath, came to Cottesmore for a few weeks on an exchange of crews to give 14 OTU crews the benefits of their experience. He told them that to be a successful bomber pilot they needed to have a high degree of skill and dash if they wanted to survive and carry out successful attacks, and that did not mean sitting up at high level in relative safety nor did it mean risking the crew's life unnecessarily. What it did mean was getting the bombs onto the target in the most expeditious way, and he expounded his method of dive bombing in the Hampden. This consisted of a 60 degree dive from 6,000 feet pulling out at 2,000 feet. He found that he could get great accuracy that way and he reckoned that he stood a reasonable chance against flak and searchlights. The only snag he had encountered was the speed that the Hampden would get up to in the final pull out was so great that several times the perspex nose of his Hampden collapsed.

Gibson had tried this technique on a raid on oil tanks in the docks at Hamburg shortly before, but on the first dive his bombs had hung up in the bomb bay to his evident fury. He had another go. He gives his own account:

'... We began to climb up again. With a load on, this was a long business, but we had to be quick because it was getting light. At last with the engines red hot we reached 5,000 feet. But

when we got there we could not find our oil tanks, as smoke from the fire had begun to blot them and everything else out. As we were circling round and round to avoid searchlights and flak I noticed a lot of balloons floating around above me - a not too pleasant sight. Suddenly on my right hand side I saw what we wanted and dived straight for them. Because the dive was practically vertical we reached the phenominal speed of 320 miles per hour, and the pull out was quite impossible, even though I put both feet on the panel, but she came out all right by using the tail trimming tabs (which they say is very bad for an aeroplane) so quickly in fact that we all blacked out'.

It is interesting to note that the comments of his crew on this manoeuvre have not been recorded for publication and indeed there is no record of dive bombing in the Hampden on the syllabus on 14 OTU during its time at Cottesmore!.

The 'Nickels' continued, sometimes with instructor crews, increasingly with students. Many were uneventful, some were not. On 8 October 1940 Flying Officer Dunlop-Mackenzie with his crew; Sergeants Dart, Graham and Crawford took off for Rouen at 0138 on a clear night. They elected to go for height and by the time they had crossed the French coast they had reached 17,000 feet. The cold was intense, fingers froze, feet became numb, and circulation seemed to congeal in their veins, but they could see the ground. They released their leaflets over Rouen and then turned for home and then they saw an airfield about six miles west south west of Dieppe and were able to make a good run and release. They felt confident that their bombs had hit the target. The cold was more than just a nuisance on some occasions, as on 25 October when Flying Officer Fritiger and Sergeants Stevens, Little and Power, flying at 15,000 feet, saw ice forming on the leading edges of the wings, on the windows and gun canopies and found the tail trimmer tabs jammed. Neither leaflets nor bombs would leave the aircraft, which suddenly fell out of control. It was some thousands of feet later and ageless seconds before Fritiger regained control. Some times Cottesmore was covered in fog when the aircraft returned. On 16 October Sgt. Lauderdale's crew was diverted to Mildenhall, Pilot Officer Parry's crew was not so lucky; they got lost in the fog and crash landed at 0808 near Glapthorn Manor, north west of Oundle. On other occasions crews had the infuriating experience of finding an airfield, making a good bombing run and then finding that the bombs would not release. This happened to Flying Officer Dunlop-Mackenzie on 8 November flying with Sergeants Eastwood, Smith-Gander and Ostler. They found two airfields and made careful bombing runs on both targets, but the bombs hung up on both occasions. Their wrath turned to alarm when, over Ostend, they were suddenly blinded by a searchlight. Flying Officer Dunlop-Mackenzie flung his aircraft about the sky to try to shake it off, but one after another others caught them until they reckoned they were coned by 24 searchlights. They somehow escaped to tell the tale. A few months later the flak defences were not so forgiving.

On 23 December 1940, Pilot Officer Keartland flew the last 'Nickel' operation from Cottesmore; he brought his bombs back having seen no airfield on which he could legally have released them. Seen as training sorties for a training unit, the operations were invaluable; crews flew with live weapons for the first time in a threatening environment, in all conditions and they survived - no crews were lost. As offensive operations, very little significant damage was done. It would be 16 months before Cottesmore aircraft were called upon to fly operationally in quite a different style and force.

Lights in the gloom.
There were lighter moments at Cottesmore during that grim Winter. For some time there had been an intention to form a station band. It became a reality on 18 December 1940 when to great excitement among the enthusiasts the instruments arrived: six cornets, two horns, two baritones, two euphoniums, two tenor trombones, one bass trombone, two bass's, and most magnificent, the drums and cymbals. And what a fine sight they made, as they made their debut on the first fine day of the year. The unit diary

made no reference to their expertise, though the stirring works of John Phillip Sousa reverberated in the hangars and recreation rooms for many months.

1941 was not a good year for Cottesmore or for Bomber Command as a whole, primarily because of the failure of the aircraft expansion programme. This was due almost entirely to the delays in the new generation of heavy bombers reaching the squadrons. All of the new types had at the very least, teething troubles: the Manchester with its insufficiently developed Rolls-Royce Vulture engines was probably the most serious, but the Stirling had a very limited service ceiling (due to its short wing span designed for accommodation in pre-war hangars) and a bomb bay which limited the heaviest bomb to 4,000 pounds; the Halifax had tail wheel and hydraulic problems. Some of the faults were ironed out during development, some were not. The Lancaster was the exception, it was the one bright spot; and it became the most successful bomber of the war. The first RAF aircraft was delivered to 44 Squadron at Waddington on Christmas Eve 1941.

The problem affected Cottesmore, and the other OTUs, primarily in the organisation of courses. In order to man the expected flow of aircraft (which did not materialise), larger numbers of aircrew arrived and to accommodate them the duration of courses was reduced. This resulted in the graduation of crews who were not so well trained as they might have been and, by November 1941, led to the production of a large surplus of aircrew.

Among the influx of aircrew to Cottesmore were some who had already made their name, and others who were destined to do so. Sgt. Hannah VC, the quiet young man from Paisley in Scotland, was posted in as a Wireless Operator Instructor. He won his VC for extinguishing a fire in his 83 Squadron Hampden following an attack on the invasion barges at Antwerp in September 1940. The injuries he received that day were further exacerbated in two serious crashes on instructor duties at Cottesmore. In May he was flying on a night exercise in Anson R9692. The sortie was uneventful until the aircraft had returned to the circuit and had completed two practice circuits. On the approach for the final landing something caused the pilot to overshoot. The aircraft struck some telegraph wires; somehow the pilot dragged the aircraft clear and put it down on the airfield still in one piece. The crew walked, a little shakily, away from it. It was soon clear that Hannah's accumulated injuries had affected him more profoundly than had first been thought. During his time on the OTU, he met and married a local girl. He was invalided from the RAF in December 1942 and died of tuberculosis in 1947.

Another VC at Cottesmore in 1941 was Flight Lieutenant R A B Learoyd who won his decoration on the night of 12/13 August 1940 when five Hampdens, flown by crews from 49 and 83 Sqns, attacked an aqueduct on the Dortmund-Ems Canal. Learoyd was the last of the five to attack, he came in when the defences were well and truly stirred up. In the face of blinding searchlights and intense flak, his bomb aimer placed his bombs so accurately that the canal was blocked for 10 days with the result that the movement of barges from the Rhineland to the invasion ports fell seriously behind schedule. His badly damaged aircraft managed to limp back to Scampton.

Flying Officer Leslie Manser had not yet achieved fame when he passed through the OTU at Cottesmore. He was another unassuming young man who flew the Hampden by the book at Cottesmore and who was posted to 50 Squadron at Swinderby at the completion of the course. He had not been there long when the Squadron exchanged its Hampdens for the new and vastly more sophisticated Manchester. It seemed properly heated and comfortable for the crew of seven (two pilots, navigator, bomb aimer, wireless operator, mid-upper and rear gunners) after the icy Hampden. They soon found that it had grave faults: the engines were unreliable, the coolant pipes proved lethally vulnerable to shrapnel, the undercarriage was weak and it could not reach the Hampdens service ceiling of 20,000 feet. Flight Lieutenant Manser captained one of 50 Squadron's Manchesters which took part in the first RAF 1,000 bomber raid of the war on Cologne on the night of 30 May 1942. His aircraft was hit over the stricken city and began to lose height as he turned for home. He held the aircraft steady for as long as possible before he gave the order to the crew to abandon the aircraft. One by one they went until the engineer (who had replaced the second pilot) held out his parachute for him. Manser waved him away. He was still in the aircraft when it hit the ground with a blinding flash, still within the sound of the guns. He was posthumously awarded the VC.

Squadron Leader J D Nettleton, a South African, was posted to 44 Squadron at Waddington after leaving Cottesmore. He won his VC on 17 April 1942, in Lancaster R5508, when he led 12 Lancasters of 44 and 97 squadrons on an attack on the Maschinenfabrik Augsburg-Nürnberg Aktiengesellschaft submarine diesel engine factory deep into Germany at Augsburg. The 1,250 miles unescorted, low-level, daylight attack by the first few Lancaster bombers to become operational was hazardous in the extreme. Four aircraft were shot down by fighters before they reached the Paris area on the way out, the remaining two reached Augsburg in the golden light of a sunny evening and flew into a hail of flak which accounted for Flying Officer A J Garwell's aircraft soon after he had released his bombs; leaving Nettleton's the only 44 Squadron crew to survive. Of the six 97 Squadron Lancasters that had somehow miraculously missed the fighters on the way out, two were destroyed in the target area by the ground defences. All four of the surviving aircraft that returned to Waddington were full of holes. Squadron Leader Nettleton's citation spoke of his skilled airmanship, leadership, courage and determination. He failed to return from a raid on Turin on the night of 12/13 July 1943.

Pilot Officer Harold (Mickey) Martin, from Edgecliffe Australia, passed through the gates of Cottesmore on 2 August 1941 to begin his operational training. After the war, Group Captain Leonard Cheshire VC, Commanding Officer of 617 Squadron and one of the most distinguished RAF bomber pilots himself, was to say this of him:

> The backbone of the squadron (617) were Martin, Munro, McCarthy and Shannon, and of all of them by far the greatest was Martin. He was not a man to worry about administration then (though I think he is now), but as an operational pilot I consider him greater than Gibson, and indeed the greatest that the air force ever produced. I have seen him do things that I, for one, would never have looked at ... I learned all I knew of this low flying game from Mick. He showed me what you could do by coming in straight and hard and low, and I never saw him make a mistake ... Mick Martin was the greatest bomber pilot of the war'. (Quoted by Peter Firkins in The Golden Eagles - St George Books Perth, West Australia 1980).

'Micky' Martin was recognised with the award of a DSO and bar, DFC and two bars. Many however, received no medals.

Flying Officer Stanley Carter was one such. He gained a civil pilot's licence before the war but when war came he was considered to be too old to be a pilot and so became an air gunner, serving on 14 OTU at Cottesmore in 1940 and 1941. He was posted to 83 Squadron at Scampton in March 1941 where he flew 10 combat missions before he was shot down over Dusseldorf on 30 June. His total flying was 186 hours. Fortunately, Lord Haw Haw, the Britisher who broadcast for the German radio services announced a few days later that an injured Flying Officer Carter was a POW and would take no more part in the war.

Many of the new generation of aircrew passing through Cottesmore in 1941 were volunteers from overseas, and the Commonwealth Countries. These young men were among the very best of their generation and they were offering themselves for arguably the most hazardous of all wartime careers. The proportion of overseas aircrew may be seen from the following Bomber Command figures for aircrew killed throughout the war: RAF 38,462 (69.2% of the whole), RCAF 9,919 (17.8%), RAAF 4,050 (7.3%), RNZAF 1679 (3%), other Allied Air Forces 1,463 (2.8%). Many of these aircrew had their initial flying training in Canada, Australia, Southern Rhodesia, South Africa, India, New Zealand, The Middle East, USA and the Bahamas in the Empire Training Scheme begun in April 1940. Those destined for Cottesmore arrived at the smoke blackened Grantham railway station and no doubt compared the grey and chilly clouds with their own sunny skies as they piled their kit bags and gas masks onto the awaiting vehicle that trundled up the ancient Roman road - Ermine Street, (then the Great North Road), south towards Rutland and Cottesmore; or else they came north to Stamford, the graceful old town full of Georgian and Queen Anne houses, and where they might have noted for future reference, The George, the old coaching inn. From here The Great North Road led them through the old Roman fort town of North Casterton, and northwards to the Ram Jam Inn, through Greetham village to Cottesmore airfield.

'Faithful Annie...'

Many of these student crews experienced their first flying at Cottesmore in the Avro Anson which was proving to be a rugged and reliable trainer after an indifferent start as a coastal reconnaissance aircraft. It had none of the flying vices of the Hereford and Hampden and gradually it began to live up to its service nickname of 'Faithful Annie'. As new items of equipment arrived, or new techniques developed, they tended to be tried out first on the Ansons. In January 1941, the OTU received a new type of Marconi General Purpose Wireless set. They found it a big improvement over the earlier equipment and soon the Station History records the occasional 'good show' as an operator produced a praiseworthy effort. Thus on 31 March 1941 Sgt. Calderwood, who was a WOP/AG on No 22 Course acquitted himself well on his first night trip on Anson R9748. Cottesmore weather suddenly dropped below limits and the aircraft was first recalled and then diverted. Calderwood coolly homed the aircraft to Cottesmore, switching to radio-telephony (R/T) for instructions, then he homed to Wyton finally carrying out an accurate ZZ approach from which the aircraft landed safely.

With the Ansons, the crews were at last able to get to grips with astro navigation. The aircraft were fitted with astro domes in August 1941 so that the navigators could take realistically accurate shots of the stars for the first time. They could hang the sextant from a fitting so that the weight was supported allowing them to concentrate on keeping the star in the centre of the bubble. Pilots were briefed of the importance of accurate, steady flying during the duration of the shots. An alteration of a degree in heading could throw the shot hopelessly out. The Anson flew right through the war and continued afterwards as a trainer until the last was delivered from Avro's Yeadon factory at the end of May 1952, the 8,138th to be built in Britain (a further 2,882 were build in Canada). It finally retired from the RAF in June 1968.

Not all aircraft returned to Cottesmore successfully during that Spring and Summer, and April 1941 was a particularly trying month. On 8 April two Hampdens were on a night exercise over the Grimsthorpe bombing range when one of them, Pilot Officer Crump's aircraft, P1240, lost an engine. The wing dropped but Crump did manage to crash land in a field, half a mile from Little Bytham, saving his crew. A few moments later an enemy intruder, probably a Junkers Ju88, was reported in the area. As a consequence, Cottesmore immediately switched off its lights. Shortly afterwards the other Hampden, P2092, captained by Sgt.Holborrow and crewed by Pilot Officer Cochrane and Sgt.Cunningham, crashed on the railway line at Little Bytham killing all the crew. The next day 9 April, Hampden P1176, flown by Pilot Officer S J Beard, lost the starboard engine on take-off, the torque of the port engine swung the aircraft violently to the right tearing off the undercarriage. Later the same day, Squadron Leader G Avis had just become airborne in Hampden L4193 when the starboard engine started to vibrate, the airscrew suddenly flew off and the engine caught fire. Showing great skill he somehow managed to control the stricken aircraft during the critical seconds necessary to turn the aircraft and put it back down on the airfield. Even though the undercarriage was still retracted when they hit the grass, they all survived. That evening Cottesmore was on the receiving end of two air raid attacks, at 2203 and 2225 during which incendiary bombs were dropped. A hangar was hit, but the fires were kept under control and little damage done. On 11 April at 0230 the raiders returned again and for an hour, flares, incendiaries and high explosive bombs were dropped from about 10,000 feet. Although one bomb fell on the bomb dump, no significant damage was done.

On the evening of 17 April a raider came in low on a daring attack on Woolfox Lodge while the circuit was full of Cottesmore aircraft, he machine-gunned the flare path and dropped seven HE bombs, one of which fell on the runway. April 1941 ended with the loss of 10 aircraft.

This may seem to be an appalling accident rate but over a long period it was certainly no worse than at the other OTUs. Official RAF figures show that 5,327 aircrew were killed and 3,113 were injured in RAF training accidents between 1939 and 1945. Yet the OTUs managed to turn out the crews at the planned rate. In order to do this, the ground crews faced a herculean task. Aircraft that appeared at first glance to be totally beyond repair, frequently flew again after only a few days of feverish activity in the hangars. Figures from the Station ORB give some idea of the serviceability. In November 1940 the aircraft state was:

	On Charge	Serviceable	Unserviceable	Disposal /write off
Hampden	31	15	12	4
Hereford	16	2	14	0
Anson	28	12	12	4

Two months later, in January 1941, the picture was very much the same:

Hampden	31.4	15.7	11.7
Hereford	16	2	14
Anson	29.4	18.6	7.1

By March 1942, after the removal of the Herefords, we find some different types arriving to supplement the Hampdens most of which had been handed down from the front line squadrons after the stuffing had been knocked out of them:

Hampdens - 47, Ansons - 14, Oxfords - 8, Lysanders - 2 (for target towing), Tiger Moth - 1.

Group Captain A P Ritchie AFC took over command of Cottesmore in September 1941, and an event of even more significance both to Cottesmore and Bomber Command as a whole, a few months later in February 1942 Air Chief Marshal Sir Arthur Harris, KCB, OBE, AFC became Commander-in-Chief (C-in-C) Bomber Command.

The low ebb of fortune...

Bomber Command's fortunes were at a low ebb when Harris took over, indeed the entire British War Effort at the turn of 1942/43 was far from encouraging. Bomber Command seemed to have made no effective reply to the Luftwaffe Blitz on London, Coventry and the other British cities. London had been attacked by 410 aircraft on 15 October 1941, 473 on 19 March 1942, 685 on 16 April, the attacking force of 712 on 19 April was greater than the entire establishment of Bomber Command at the time.

Four hundred RAF aircraft took off to attack a variety of targets on the night of 7/8 November 1941. Thirty-seven failed to return (9.25%) but even more alarming was the fact that this figure represented 25.87% of those aircraft that had actually reached their targets. Such losses meant that Harris had inherited a force that had not grown significantly for two years. On the day he took over, he wrote:

There were 378 aircraft serviceable with crews, and only 69 of these were heavy bombers. About 50 aircraft in the force were not even medium bombers, but the light bombers of 2 Group ... In effect this meant that we had an average force of 250 medium and 50 heavy bombers, until such time as the Command really began to expand.'

He had though, at least one good card to play: the first of the new navigation aids, GEE, invented by R J Dippy came into large scale production in March 1942. This was a radar system from which the navigator could get a fix by timing the pulse signals received from three ground stations which appeared on a cathode ray screen. It was very accurate over the UK although, naturally, it became less so the farther away from the transmitters; the navigators could however, by getting a series of fixes; early on, find an accurate wind and so improve their track keeping considerably. Sometimes at extreme range they might only be able to get a single position line but that was much better than hitherto, it was however strictly a navigation aid and not a bombing aid as had been originally hoped.

The C-in-C decided that his force required a spectacular demonstration of its power in order to restore morale. There were no longer any constraints placed in the way of targets. Indeed, after the civilian population had taken the brunt of the Blitz, there was a tacit thirst for revenge. He directed large scale attacks on Lubeck and Rostock on four consecutive nights; both were coastal towns and were therefore relatively easy to find and attack. The raids were successful. But Harris wanted to make his mark by attacking a major German city with the greatest concentration of aircraft ever conceived.

The plan to use every available Bomber Command asset, under the code name 'MILLENNIUM', went ahead with Churchill's blessing. It appealed to his sense of drama. The Admiralty was totally unimpressed with the idea; they were engaged in a desperate, life and death struggle against the U-boats and refused to allow their precious Coastal Command aircraft to be used for what they considered to be a gimmick. Flying Training Command offered a few aircraft but nearly all came from Bomber Command's own resources: 675 front line bombers and 367 from the OTUs, including 30 from Cottesmore. Ground crew worked around the clock to complete major work in the hangars, making unserviceable aircraft serviceable and bringing training aircraft up to operational standard. The feverish activity of the engineers and relative inactivity of the aircrew convinced the airmen that an enterprise of great moment was afoot. The Cottesmore armourers had for over a year been dealing mainly with practice bombs; they now began to trundle 250 pound HE bombs and incendiaries from the bomb dump, and winch them up into the bomb bays of the aircraft. Final orders were complete and the force stood ready waiting for the full moon on 30th May. The weather in England suddenly improved after 10 indifferent days. Rutland in late May sunshine is at its best, but the aircrew called in from the surrounding villages did not notice it.

Target Cologne

The forecast for Germany was doubtful. The primary target was Hamburg, the great port where 100 U-boats were built every year. Dudley Saward, in The Bomber's Eye (Cassell 1959), described the scene at Bomber Command's Headquarters at High Wycombe. After listening to the Met Officer's forcast: *The C-in-C moved at last. ..... He turned to the SASO, his face still expressionless: "The 1,000 Plan tonight" His finger was pressing on Cologne.'*

The 30 Cottesmore crews were composed of instructors, men who had completed tours on operations and the most highly trained of the students. At the briefing when it was announced that there would be over 1,000 aircraft over the target within 90 minutes there was a murmur of concern, the thought of collision instantly in their minds. When told that the boffins had calculated the chances as one in a thousand, disbelief prompted a hostile shuffling of feet. It turned out to be an accurate assessment. One of Cottesmore's Hampdens: P5321 provided the feared statistic. It collided with a Halifax; Squadron Leader Falconer, the captain survived. His crew, Flight Sgt.Holmes, Sgt.Knowling and Pilot Officer Little did not. The crews were told of the importance of timing and accurate navigation, reminded of strict R/T discipline and the need for extreme care in taxying - all 30 would be airborne within 34 minutes. The entire force would be led by GEE equipped aircraft of 1 and 3 Groups and it was hoped that their flares and fires would guide in the main force. The Station Commander, Group Captain A Leach MC wished them luck, and they walked from the briefing room into a glorious Summer evening.

Flight Lieutenant K G Tew led the Cottesmore force off the ground at 2243 hours. One by one the Hampdens lumbered into position and rolled off across the airfield trying to keep out of the slipstream of the aircraft ahead; and so it went on at about one minute intervals until Pilot Officer Gillies lifted Hampden P1204 off the ground at 2317 and the roar of engines slowly became a murmur in the east. One of the last aircraft to get airborne was Hampden P5312 captained by Pilot Officer McLoughlin who found the pilot's compass unserviceable. He struggled on for a while but realised that accurate flying was impossible and so he turned back.

Flight Lieutenant Tew, flying at 11,000 feet, skirted the known heavy flak around the Munchen Gladbach area and approached Cologne in the pale moonlight, only a few minutes behind the leaders. There was only a little cirrus cloud, high in the sky, and he could see the ribbon of the River Rhine and the bridges across it quite clearly. His bomb aimer released the two 250 pound general purpose (GP) bombs and his four packs of 90 4 pound incendiary bombs, at one minute to midnight over the centre of the city. As the later aircraft approached the target they found it bathed in a red glow; the higher flying aircraft could see others below reflected in the flickering lights of the fires, the flashes from the flak batteries and the wandering searchlights contributed to the impression of some wild inferno. As the Cottesmore aircraft flew over the target the crews noted the situation for their reports: 'target easily identified in bright moonlight - target identified by cathedral and bridges - by large fires and the river - large fires made identification certain - no difficulty in identifying target by the light of widespread fires - huge fires made identification of target a simple matter,' and so on. Of all the Cottesmore crews who reported, only one failed to attack the primary target. Flight Sgt.Hill was one of the earlier aircraft airborne and for some reason did not find Cologne, but the moonlight and the good visibility revealed the airfield at Haamstede so he bombed that.

The AOC 3 Group, Air Vice-Marshal Baldwin, who was flying as a passenger in one of his group's Wellingtons, marvelled at the sight of Cologne apparently ablaze from end to end. Micky Martin, then a member of 50 Squadron, arrived over the target at H hour plus 45 minutes; he could see the sky ahead ablaze with light. He circled the city three times wondering if he should take his bombs back, as it already appeared to be devastated. He finally dropped them on the ruins of the railway station from 4,000 feet. It was said that no man who was there ever forgot the sight of Cologne that night.

There was already a pale light in the eastern sky when the first aircraft touched down at Cottesmore, to be met by little knots of men who had been sitting around all night waiting and smoking. The sun was up as Pilot Officer Rickman landed at 0500, after 6 hours and 50 minutes in the air. Apart from the Hampden which collided with the Halifax, two other Cottesmore Hampden's failed to return. L4173 crashed at Horsham St Faith killing the crew; and P2116 was presumed lost. Forty-one aircraft were missing from the entire force. This was deemed an 'acceptable' 3.93% of the total, considering the perfect weather conditions which, whilst assisting the bombers, also helped the German defences. The Official History estimated that 36 factories ceased production altogether and 70 were reduced to half their normal output; the loss of one month's production was a reasonable supposition.

There was also a price to pay amongst the German civilian population. Cologne records listed 3,330 buildings destroyed, 2,090 seriously damaged and 7,420 lightly damaged. Of the 469 people killed, 411 were civilians, the other 58 were military, mostly from the flak units. Part of the concept of the area bombing had been an attack upon the morale of the civilian population but the citizens of Cologne displayed the same stoic qualities that Londoners had shown throughout the Blitz, and like the Londoners they quickly set about repairing what was repairable.

Harris immediately began remustering the survivors of those 601 Wellingtons, 131 Halifaxes, 88 Stirlings, 79 Hampdens, 73 Lancasters, 46 Manchesters and 28 Whitleys. He intended to use them on another maximum effort as soon as conditions permitted. On the night of 1/2 June he launched 957 aircraft at the more difficult target of Essen; 27 came from Cottesmore. This time the weather was not clear; there was almost full cover of cloud at 8,000 feet in the target area in addition to the customary Essen haze.

Flight Lieutenant Tew was again the first Cottesmore aircraft to take off - at 2247 hours, and like many of the other crews he could not say with certainty that he had identified the target. Some, like Sgt.Hamer's crew found it by following the River Rühr, others by the glare from fires. This was not always a wise thing to do because the defenders were adept at lighting fires away from the targets for precisely this reason. Flight Lieutenant Salazar's crew was below cloud at 7,000 feet and he dropped his bombs on a 'huge fire' and was hit by the flak for his pains but, managed to limp home safely. Squadron Leader Barnard identified the target by the light of flares through a gap in the clouds; he was at 12,000 feet, Squadron Leader Petty attacked a large fire which seemed to be surrounded by a large concentration of flak. Pilot Officer Daniel saw nothing and released his bombs on ETA, Flight Sgt.Hill through a glow in the cloud, as did most of the others. Flight Sgt.Letford's aircraft was at 10,000 feet when it was struck by an incendiary bomb dropped by an aircraft above him, badly injuring one of his crew. They tried to make him as comfortable as possible in an aircraft with a gaping hole in it, but even in June at 10,000 feet at night the cold was intense and soon after the aircraft landed back at Cottesmore, he died. All except three of the Hampdens released their bombs on what the crews thought was the target area; none were able to observe results. Of the three who didn't make it, one landed at Coltishall outbound due to engine trouble, one returned early with compass troubles and Flying Officer Biggane did not get airborne from Cottesmore due to an engine fault. All Cottesmore aircraft returned safely, although 31 were lost from the force as a whole. Subsequent analysis revealed that the bombing had been very scattered, indeed Oberhausen, Duisburg and Mühlheim all reported more damage than Essen. The main target, the famous Krupp works, seemed to have suffered no damage. The next day, Bomber Command reported that widespread attacks on targets in the Rühr had been carried out. German radio did not recognise the target as Essen either and instead reported widespread raids over Western Germany. There was clearly still an urgent requirement for an accurate bombing aid. The first of these, OBOE, did not make its operational debut until 20 December 1942 and the second, H2S, did not enter service until 30 January 1943, after Cottesmore had completed its operational career.

Cottesmore was able to revert to its primary role for a few days, until the night of 25/26 June, when Harris once more called on his training groups to assist the main force in a maximum effort. Every type of aircraft in the Command was employed including Bostons and the new Mosquitos of 2 Group. This time 1,003 aircraft were dispatched to Bremen of which Cottesmore supplied 24. The targets were the U-boat construction yards, the A G Weser shipyard, the docks and the Focke-Wulf aircraft factory. For this attack the bombing period was cut to 65 minutes. On the face of it Bremen, on the River Weser, should have been an easier target to find than Essen, but once again the weather intervened. A layer of cloud lay over the target during the day but Met forecast that a fresh wind from the west would clear it away in time for the attack. The wind, if it came, dropped during the evening and the cover was still there when the bombers arrived. The early GEE equipped aircraft were however able to fix themselves right up to the target area and were able to start a series of fires, the glow from which drew many of the following aircraft. All except one of the Cottesmore aircraft attacked this beacon of light. The losses to the force as a whole were 48 aircraft including four which came down in the sea off the English Coast and from which all but two crew members were rescued. These were the highest losses so far to the Command in one attack. They may be partially explained by the extra 200 miles round trip, although the primary reason was the increasing efficiency of the German defences. Flight Lieutenant Salazar and crew was the one loss sustained by the Cottesmore force. 91 (Operational Training) Group suffered the most grievously in the attack, with the loss of 23 of the 198 Whitleys and Wellingtons that took off; 21 of these were flown by trainee crews.

The attack on Bremen was much more successful than that on Essen. The Bremen Stadtarchiv reported that a strengthening wind had fanned many of the fires increasing the extent of the damage and leaving whole areas in ruins although the shipyard and the Focke-Wulf factory were only partially damaged. One 4,000 pound bomb dropped by a 5 Group Lancaster hit and destroyed an assembly shop, damage was also reported to the Atlas Werke, the Vulcan shipyard, the Norddeutsche Hutte, the Korff Refinery and to two large dockside warehouses. Bremen was the third and last of the '1,000 bomber' raids. In the space of four weeks, Harris and his men had delivered an assault of a magnitude that seemed an impossibility when he had taken over five months earlier. It served as a warning of what was possible and provided a propaganda coup in the face of urgent demands for decisive action by the Russians and Americans, but at a cost of 134 aircraft and over 770 aircrew. The scale of attacks for the remainder of 1942 was reduced and the OTUs returned to their primary role of training, although they were called upon from time to time to provide aircraft for the larger scale raids that followed during the year.

On the night of 31 July/1 August, 630 aircraft were tasked to attack Dusseldorf. This was the first raid on which more than 100 Lancasters were to participate. 14 OTU, still training with Hampdens were tasked for this raid, by 92 (Operational Training) Group, to provide 30 of the Group's 54 Hampdens. These old 'heaps' may have demonstrated limitations, but they had strengths as well; good range, endurance and the ability to gain a reasonable height.

Cottesmore lost three aircraft on this raid with 92 Group losing 11 of it's 105 aircraft, a rate of 10.5%. Heavy damage was done to Dusseldorf's industrial production but by no means all the bombs fell on the target. Nevertheless from about this time Harris came under pressure from Bomber Operations Directorate to strike at more precise targets rather than the area bombing for which the aids and techniques then in use, made more practicable.

Dusseldorf was attacked again on 10/11 September 1942, this time by 479 aircraft - 242 Wellingtons, 89 Lancasters, 59 Halifaxes, 28 Hampdens and 14 Whitleys. Cottesmore provided 20 aircraft. The recently formed Pathfinder Force, commanded by Air Commodore D C T Bennett, led the raid and (probably for the first time) successfully marked the target using 'Pink Pansies'. These were markers carried in converted 4,000 pound bomb casings. This elite force carried the hopes of many for more accurate bombing of pin point targets until the new bombing aids of OBOE and H2S arrived on the scene. Heavy damage to Dusseldorf and the neighbouring town of Neuss was inflicted. The local report listed 39 industrial firms in Dusseldorf and 13 in Neuss damaged so that all production ceased for various periods. Several Cottesmore aircraft were plagued with engine trouble. Four turned back early

L7850, a Vickers Wellington Ic, after crashing into Exton Park whilst on approach to Cottesmore on 2 December 1942. *(Photo: R Bonser)*

with engine malfunctions. Sgt.Cran attacked Walcheren when his engine misbehaved and Sgt.Berthiaume did not reach the primary target either due to a fault. Sgt.Campen attacked but had to force land at Chislet Marshes in Kent on his return. The old Hampdens were clearly beginning to feel their age and the effect of rough treatment.

Cottesmore was called upon twice more in September. On the 13th, 17 of its Hampdens were part of a force of 446 aircraft on another attack on Bremen in which the Lloyd Dynamo Works was put out of action for two weeks and part of the Focke-Wulf factory destroyed. The Bremen report listed five nearly completed aircraft destroyed and three damaged as well as cultural and historical buildings, for there was no possibility of discrimination in this form of warfare. The civilian population responded in its usual way. Bremen Stadtarchiv's report noted Gauleiter Wegener's announcement in the Bremer Zeitung: 'The Fuhrer has specifically instructed me to express to you all his admiration and appreciation for your bravery and disciplined behaviour.' It adds, with some relief, that Bomber Command now left Bremen alone for the next five months (Quoted by Middlebrook and Everitt in The Bomber Command War Diaries). All but 4 of Cottesmore's aircraft located and bombed the target and of the 21 aircraft that were lost, one came from 14 OTU.

The C-in-C called upon the support of his OTUs for a final effort on the Krupp Works at Essen on 16 September. Cottesmore provided 12 aircraft and although the bombing was officially described as scattered it was estimated that more damage was done during this attack than in any preceding ones on Essen. The Krupp Works was hit by 15 HE bombs and by a crashing bomber loaded with incendiaries. Other towns in the area, in particular Bochum, were damaged. Although 39 aircraft were lost all Cottesmore's aircraft returned to base, but one aircraft crashed on the airfield killing three of the crew and seriously injuring the fourth. This was a painful end to the career of the Hampden in Bomber Command. It never flew on operations again although it continued for some time as a torpedo bomber with Coastal Command.

The 151 sorties on the seven major raids by the Cottesmore aircraft between May and September cost nine aircraft and the death of 23 aircrew. This makes a sobering comparison with the 63 aircrew who were killed during training in 1942 while turning out 1,047 pilots, navigators, wireless operators and air gunners for the main squadrons.

Instances of heroism displayed by the aircrew who were trained at Cottesmore are well documented. For those who served on the ground there was less call for that sort of courage, nevertheless, a brief note appeared in Group Routine Order No 12 dated 23 February 1942 commending Flying Officer R Park, a Photographic Officer on 14 OTU, for rescuing the crew of a Hampden which crashed during a night cross country exercise. The aircraft had burst into flames and the cockpit cover had jammed trapping the crew. The order laconically observed:'*Flying Officer Park managed to release all four crew and get them to safety*'. The details were left to the imagination.

The Vickers Wellington.

As more and more Lancasters, Halifaxes and Stirlings joined the main force, more Wellingtons were freed to join the OTUs and many found their way to Cottesmore. By the end of September 1942, 14 OTUs strength stood at 36 Hampdens, 18 Wellingtons, 9 Ansons, 2 Lysanders, 1 Oxford and 1 Defiant. The last of the Hampdens departed in December and when the new Station Commander, Group Captain S Graham MC arrived to take over in January 1943, his force consisted almost exclusively of Wellingtons, with 52 on strength plus the Defiant. The Wellington, nicknamed the Wimpey, after Popeye's portly friend Mr J Wellington Wimpey, had been in service since October 1938 and was the mainstay of Bomber Command for the first three years of the war. Designed by Dr Barnes Wallis, it had an unusual lattice design (first used in the Vickers Wellesley - Cottesmore's first aircraft), known as a geodetic construction which was both light and strong - a sort of 'strength through spinach' arrangement, according to some of the crews who flew them. Over this a fabric cover was stretched, which proved to be very rugged and able to withstand heavy battle damage. The Wimpey was also a durable aircraft with sweet sounding 1,000hp Bristol Pegasus engines (later 1,500hp Bristol Hercules engines), flying right through the war and continuing on as a navigation trainer until 1953. A Wellington is displayed in the RAF Museum at Hendon, another, N2980 which ditched on New Year's Eve 1940 was exhumed from Loch Ness in 1985 and is now being patiently reassembled. 11,461 Wellingtons were built and at one time they equipped no less than 25 of the OTUs.

The Wellington had a fine record of service but generally speaking, those on the OTUs suffered from the same major problems as the Hampdens; they had been so well used on the squadrons that many of them were worn out and almost inevitably the high training accident rate continued. An incident at Cottesmore on 31 March 1943 illustrated the type of problem experienced at the time, and the response to such emergencies. A Wellington AD628(M), piloted by Sgt. Humphrey, made a normal approach and landing in poor visibility but swung violently after touchdown, colliding with another Wellington X9944 in front of C Hangar. Both aircraft burst into flames threatening the hangar and four other aircraft inside. The Station Commander, Group Captain Graham, led a rescue party into the hangar saving three injured airmen and dragging out the four Wellingtons despite injuries which he received from a bomb aboard AD628 which exploded wrecking some offices. After treatment in sick quarters, he returned to the scene and directed the fire fighters until the blaze was under control. For his gallantry and leadership in a potentially catastrophic situation, he was awarded the George Medal.

In May 1943, Cottesmore, Woolfox Lodge and Saltby were chosen as storage bases for 96 Airspeed Horsa gliders in preparation for the Allied airborne assault across the channel in June 1944. By 12 July there were 32 Horsas at Cottesmore to join the powered aircraft and the airfield was becoming a little congested. Therefore, on 1 August, 14 OTU began to move from Cottesmore and Saltby (Cottesmore's Satellite) to Market Harborough, in order for work to begin on the construction of hardened runways, the move being completed by 10 August.

CHAPTER TWO

The Americans arrive!

44 Troop Carrier Squadron at Cottesmore in 1944 *(Photo: Major Lee Ross)*

On 24 November 1942 the Chief of the Air Staff, Air Chief Marshal Sir Charles Portal, and the Chiefs of Staff framed their objectives for 1943. Firstly they aimed to render material assistance to Russia, second to prepare for the invasion of Europe and thirdly to soften up North West Europe by bombing (Official History, Webster and Franklin).

Cottesmore was to feature in the second of these objectives. But first, in order to prepare for the heavier aircraft that were coming into service it was necessary to construct hardened runways, perimeter tracks and hardstandings; to this end the airfield was placed on a Care and Maintenance basis on 10 August 1943. At the same time units of the United States Army Air Force (USAAF) were beginning to arrive in this country and the Grantham/Rutland area was chosen as a suitable base for their operations. During September 1943 a Bomber Command unit called the Air Support Division Substitution Unit (ASDSU) was formed to liaise with and assist the American Forces. On 8 September the US HQ Troop Carrier Command (TCC) took over Cottesmore airfield, which now became known as USAAF Station 489, and for the next few months it was to experience many comings and goings as the Americans got their act together. The HQ soon became the IXth TCC and on 17 October, 198 officers and 1,141 enlisted men of the 50th Troop Carrier Wing (TCW) HQ and the 434th Troop Carrier Group (TCG) and HQ arrived. The 50th TCW moved out to Bottesford, Leicestershire and the 434th TCG to Fulbeck, Lincs, to make room for them. On 19 October the 2008 Engineer Aviation Fire Platoon and the 459th Service Group arrived displacing the IXth TCC HQ. The next day the 33rd and 85th Air Depot Groups arrived. These were all ground support units preparing for the arrival of the 316th TCG consisting of numbers 36, 37, 44 and 45 Troop Carrier (TC) Squadrons equipped with C-47 (Skytrain) and a small number of C-53 (Skytrooper) aircraft, which were operating in Italy supporting the advancing Anglo American and Commonwealth forces.

The ubiqutous Dakota.

The DC3, C-47, C-53 and Dakota (RAF version) turned out to be the most celebrated and durable of all transport aircraft. It was first rolled out of a hangar in Santa Monica, California on 14 December 1935; it served in every battle zone during the war and was the mainstay of RAF and USAAF transport squadrons for many years. Of the 10,655 built, 700 were still flying world wide 50 years after its debut, an incredible record. The Skytrains and Skytroopers of the 316th TCG were to be used as troop and cargo carriers, and later, glider tugs.

32

The Anglo American Forces first landed in Sicily in July 1943 and quickly moved onto the mainland. The 316th TCG was based at Mazara and Castelvetrano in Sicily supporting the advancing ground forces, carrying troops, supplies and evacuating casualties between the allied bases in Sicily, Southern Italy and Tunisia.

Many great cities in Northern Europe had already by this time been devastated by air attack. Now it was Italy's turn. The armies were sweeping through a land that had seen the flowering of the Renaissance, a land full of treasures. Commanders on both sides were faced by terrible decisions. As John Terraine remarked in 'The Mighty Continent' BBC 1974: 'The destruction of great cities with their material wealth and industry was all too familiar; but in Italy almost every little town, every village church, every hillside palazzo might contain some priceless or venerated object, some work of art whose loss could never be replaced'. The Monastery at Monte Cassino was one such.

The 316th TCG's last operation in Italy included dropping troops of the 505th Regiment onto a zone near Agropli beside the River Sele 30 miles south east of Salerno. They started to pull out of Mazara and Castelvetrano for Cottesmore at 0855 hours on 15 February 1944, flying via El Acuina in Tunisia, Le Sonia near Oran, Algeria, Gibraltar and St Mawgan in Cornwall. By 20 February, 50 aircraft had flown into Cottesmore. All the airlifted personnel arrived at Cottesmore on 24 February. The Group's ground echelon sailed from Palermo on the British transport Monarch of Bermuda arriving at Greenock in Scotland on 18 March. With 3,700 American servicemen based at Cottesmore that Spring every conceivable type of accommodation from tents and local houses including Exton Hall, the home of the Earl of Gainsborough, were requisitioned. The new 2,000 feet long 50 feet wide hard runway was in service so that the Americans had a firm base to prepare for the final assault on Europe. They began immediately to train for this event. The 316th TCG was assigned to the 52nd TCW under the command of Brigadier General Harald L Clark who directed operations from Exton Hall. Other TCGs assigned to the Wing were the 61st at Barkston Heath, the 313th at Folkingham and the 314th at Saltby.

The 32 Horsa gliders in storage at Cottesmore since July 1943, were handed over to the 316th TCG on 17 February 1944 for possible use by them in future operations, and the re-construction work on the airfield was completed during March.

Training continued throughout the Spring including several pre-invasion practice missions. One, code named Operation Eagle took place during the evening of 11 May. The objective was to drop paratroops on a dropping zone (DZ) near Devizes in Wiltshire. Cottesmore and other American aircraft based in the Grantham/Stamford area were required to RV over March in Cambridgeshire before

LJ233, one of 32 Airspeed Horsa Gliders stored at Cottesmore during 1944.
(Photo: W Ferguson)

A typical scene at the airfield during 1944 when the Americans were in occupation
(Photo: W Ferguson)

continuing to the target zone. After the drop the same town was used as a dispersal point. It was here that two of the aircraft collided killing Major James R Farris pilot and commander of 36 TC Squadron and Lt Col Burton R Fleet commander of the 316th TCG who was flying as a passenger in the aircraft. Also killed was the pilot of the other aircraft Lt Sharper and among other passengers Chaplain Richet who had gone purely as an observer. The new Group Commander, Lt Col Harvey E Berger, took over with only a very short time to prepare for his task of leading the 316th TCG in the assault as part of the biggest invasion force ever assembled.

The invasion of Europe

A prerequisite for success in such an enormous undertaking as Operation NEPTUNE, the assault phase of Operation OVERLORD, was air supremacy. Quite suddenly in the early part of February 1944 it was achieved - though at a cost. A key factor in this success was the introduction of the first, truly long range, single engined fighter: the P-51 Mustang. At first the Mustang had been powered with an American 1,150 hp Allison engine which restricted it in practice to fighter reconnaissance because of the engine low altitude power rating, but when, in 1942 it was re-engined with a Packard 1,680 hp Merlin engine it became one of the great successes of the war. While Bomber Command were pounding away by night the American 8th Air Force bombers, escorted by P-38 (Lightning), P-47 (Thunderbolt) and Mustang fighters, carried out concerted attacks against the German fighter defences and aircraft industry. General Galland, one of the great fighter pilots of the war reported later that between January and April 1944 the Luftwaffe lost over 1,000 pilots including some of its best commanders (John Terraine The Right of the Line-Hodder and Stoughton 1985). It was enough. General Spaatz, Commander of the 8th Air Force acknowledged a loss of 210 heavy bombers and 38 fighters in the 5 peak days 20-25 February, but by this time the numbers game was on the side of the Americans. As June approached preparations at Cottesmore were well under way. Hundreds of American paratroops arrived and were accommodated in the hangars. Guards were posted and all mail held. On 3 June they started to paint broad white and black identification bands on the wings and fuselages of the C-47s and C-53s and the Waco CG-4A gliders which the Americans preferred, to the larger and heavier British Horsa gliders. Work continued all through the night and into the morning of 4 June. The vast planning that required the landing of 150,000 men and 1,500 tanks in the first 48 hours was complete, but because of a poor weather forecast in the landing area the invasion was postponed for 24 hours.

    At last, as dusk was falling on 5 June, the 1,256 paratroops of the 1st and 3rd Battalions of the 505th Parachute Infantry Regiment of the 82nd Airborne Division began to file out of the hangars and

34

moved heavily in long lines towards their aircraft. The visibility at Cottesmore was good but the forecast for the DZ was far from perfect with layers of cloud, poor visibilities and, in the Channel, choppy seas, but at this stage another 24 hours delay was unthinkable. The long lines of aircraft filled the perimeter tracks as they queued for take off. At precisely 2300 hours, the first aircraft started to roll. One after another their tails lifted, and they slowly rose into the air. The long procession began as they formed up into huge battalions in the starlit Rutland sky, the drone of their engines settling on the listeners below like a deep harmony.

The Wing assembly point was just to the east of Birmingham. There they turned on a heading for Portland Bill where they crossed the

American airmen pose in front of the Water Tower and Hangar during 1944 *(Photo: R E Oliver)*

A poor quality , but interesting photograph showing the Americans on parade at the station during 1944. *(Photo: R E Oliver)*

A C-47 of the 37 TCS with flak-damage behind the engine nacelle after it's safe return to Cottesmore. *(Photo: 316th TCG Archives)*

UK coast. From here they set course for the Cherbourg Peninsula, grateful for the clear skies, the silhouettes of aircraft above, ahead and to the sides giving reassuring friendly contact. As they crossed the Channel, fleeting shadows of supporting fighters wheeled overhead: Thunderbolts, Mustangs, and the twin-boomed Lightnings shepherding, guarding, sniffing out danger, but there seemed to be none. Then as they approached Cherbourg whisps of rapidly thickening cloud flickered by the windows, it was above, below and then they sank into it. They were aiming for a DZ just west of Saint Mere Eglise, a small town seven miles west of Utah Beach. Just on ETA the cloud parted sufficiently for the DZ to be identified, and the paratroops jumped onto their target. The formation was still intact, in good order and then they ran into some flak, machine gun and small arms fire. They took evasive action and the disciplined columns wobbled and momentarily looked ragged. Several aircraft were hit but they managed to maintain height and regained formation as they moved back into the relative safety of the channel. They returned to Cottesmore at 0500 still in formation and landed with a pale dawn in the eastern sky. Six aircraft had been damaged by flak, one crewman had been killed and others wounded but all the aircraft landed safely. The bomber crews' sacrifice had not been in vain.

One of Rutland's other airfields, the former Cottesmore satellite of Woolfox Lodge had another important role to play in the early hours of that D-day morning. 218 Squadron's Stirlings from there were carrying out a particularly intricate and vital operation. Six aircraft were flying a low level pattern over the channel, dropping window to mislead the coastal radar. At the same time 617 Squadron's Lancasters were doing the same thing further along the coast. The resulting radar reflections convinced the defenders that the approaching armadas were miles from the actual fleets, to the north of Cape d'Antifer.

The Normandy beach-head.

The objective of the airborne forces was to secure the two flanks of the invading sea-borne troops who were landing on five beaches on the south shore of the Bay of the Seine, code name Utah, Omaha, Gold, Juno and Sword. The 6th British Airborne Division had landed on the east of the bridgehead with orders to capture two bridges, destroy a coastal defence battery at Merville close to the mouth of the River Orne and destroy the bridges in the valley of the River Dives which was the next valley to the east - all

Above: Paratroops of the 82nd Airborne Division prepare to board aircraft of the 316th Troop Carrier Group at Cottesmore on 17 September 1944. *(Photo: IWM Collection)*
Below: C-47 and CG-4A's of the 37 Troop Carrier Squadron prepare for Operation 'Market' on 18 September 1944. *(Photo: A Pearcy)*

within the four hours between midnight and dawn. This they managed to do despite difficulties caused by a scattered landing. In so doing they secured the eastern flank of the bridgehead against an expected attack by the 21st German Panzer Division.

The American airborne landings on the west of the bridgehead comprising the 101st and 82nd Divisions encountered more problems and were unable to secure all their objectives. The task of the 82nd Division, part of which was carried in the Cottesmore aircraft, was to ensure that when the sea-borne troops landed at Utah Beach they would be free to move inland. Their objectives were the bridges and causeways which spanned the flooded areas in the valleys of the Rivers Merderet, Douve and Vire. The 82nd's first objective, the road junction at Sainte Mere Eglise on the main road from Cherbourg to Carentan, was safely taken, but it failed to secure the bridges over the River Merderet in the face of determined resistance from the German 91st Division.

The 101st Division, which had the same task as the 82nd Division, succeeded in all its objectives except one: the destruction of the bridges across the Vire estuary and Carentan Canal. In spite of these failures, the airborne landings achieved enough success for the main bridgehead to become established and helped to ensure the break out into Normandy.

A CG-4A pilot's view of the 316th TCG as they prepare to leave Cottesmore for Operation 'Market'. Aircraft on the right is a C-53 42-68772 of the 44 TCS. *(Photo Major Lee Ross).*

Left: Preparing a CG-4A glider. Note the specially laid out towing rope with intercom cable attached to it. *(Photo: 316 TCG archives)Right:* A C-47 getting airborne towing a CG-4A glider from Cottesmore on 18 September 1944 on Operation 'Market'. *(Photo: IWM Collection).*

The following day (D+1), 52 aircraft were again airborne from Cottesmore to re-supply the 82nd Division by parachute. This time two aircraft collided before take off, killing one of the pilots and a number of aircraft were damaged during the operation, two, including Lt Col Berger's aircraft, returned on one engine. Thirteen aircraft of 36 TC Squadron were bringing up the rear of the 316th TCG's formation when, due to poor weather over the DZ, they were ordered to turn back. One of its aircraft continued to the DZ where it ran into heavy flak which forced it to land at an emergency landing strip in France. The crew escaped but counted 27 bullet holes in their aircraft before they walked away. For its work in the invasion of Normandy the 316th TCG were awarded the Distinguished Unit Citation.

From the 8th to the 14th of June, the 316th TCG stood by to drop the British 1st Airborne Division near Evrecy, nine miles south west of Caen in Operation WILDOATS. It had been hoped to capture Caen during the first few days but this had proved to be impossible due to the unexpected resistance of the 21st Panzer Division which happened to be garrisoned in Caen much to the surprise of the attacking forces. Events were however moving quickly and by 7 June Bayeux, Creully, Douvres and Ouistreham were all taken linking up the three British/Canadian Bridgeheads, and by 12 June the 101st American Airborne Division captured Carentan closing the last gap between Omaha and Utah beaches and linking the Allied Forces together in a beach head 42 miles wide. The aircraft to drop the 1st Airborne Division paratroops were ready on the evening of 13 June when it was postponed again. The plan had changed. On 15 June it was cancelled. The Allied ground forces now forced their way across the Cotentin Peninsula to cut off and capture the port of Cherbourg. They achieved this objective on 27 June.

Above: C-53 42-68769 of 36 TCS on 17 September 1944 loads paratroops of the 82nd Airborne Division in preparation for Operation 'Market' *(Photo: W Ferguson).*
Below: A C-47 of 44 TCS tows a CG-4A glider over France enroute to Arnhem.
(Photo Major Lee Ross)

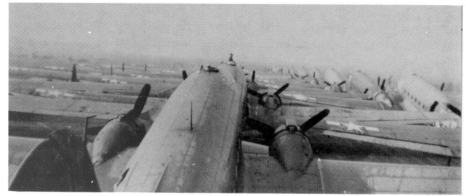

316th TCG aircraft and CG-4A gliders prepare for take-off on 18 September 1944 for Operation 'Market'. (Note the Horsa gliders parked in the centre of the airfield.)
(Photo: W. Ferguson)

The 316th TCG were now busy carrying freight and medical supplies into the battle areas and evacuating casualties. On 23 June for example, 9 aircraft from 36 TC Squadron flew to Greenham Common to load up with supplies and medical teams. They landed near St-Laurent-sur-Mer in Normandy and brought out wounded men. The 'blood runs' continued through July and into August. Then, in August, the Wing prepared to carry out three major operations ahead of the advancing Allied troops. In Operation TRANSFIGURE, on 17 August, the plan was to carry engineers of the 101st Airborne Division to a zone 26 miles south west of Paris to try to trap the German 7th Army south of that great city. Such was the speed of the advance that American tanks reached the area first and the operation was cancelled.

The second: Operation LINNET, planned for the night of 2/3 September was to carry American, British and Polish troops to a zone near Tournai in Belgium, the third was Operation COMET planned for 8 September to carry British and Polish troops to Arnhem, but rapid changes in the situation caused these too to be cancelled. Other routine operations continued; hauling fuel for U.S. 3rd Army units to airfields near Verdun (the scene of a bloody First World War battle), and delivering ammunition to the British 2nd Army near Brussels in Belgium.

Then came Operation MARKET the biggest airborne operation of the war. This bold plan was conceived to outflank German Forces in the Netherlands by crossing the River Meuse (or Maas in Flemish) at Grave, the Waal at Nijmegen and, the big prize, the Rhine at Arnhem for a decisive push on the Rühr. In order to do this with any confidence the ground forces depended on being able to use the essential bridges over those three rivers. The British 1st Airborne Division, with the 1st Polish Parachute Brigade, would take and hold them until the ground forces arrived. The 316th TCG's aircraft were assigned to drop the American 82nd Airborne Division, part of the newly formed 1st Allied Airborne Army on a DZ just east of Grave, the small town south west of Nijmegen.

The greatest aerial armada...

On 17 September 1944 Sunday morning worshippers on their way to church could hear the distant rumble of aero engines. On the airfield the biggest armada of aircraft yet seen in Rutland moved out of their dispersals and rolled towards the take off point like so many disciplined bees. There were the usual human disasters; one of the paratroopers shot himself in the foot, but insisted on continuing after treatment. At 1050 the throttles of the first of the 90 aircraft were opened wide and it began to roll down the runway with the others following closely behind. The rumble became a roar and the sky became dark with aircraft circling, forming up before turning onto a heading of 109 magnetic and as the voices

The cockpit of a CG-4A glider *(Photo: 316 TCG archives)*

swelled in the churches below, 1,362 paratroopers of the 82nd Airborne Division huddled with their equipment in the confined spaces with Brigadier General James Gavin in command and with the war correspondent Ed Morrow on hand to record the scene. Apart from one aircraft that had to land before reaching the coast to unload a paratrooper who had gone mad, they moved towards Grave with a deliberate stately discipline. They dropped their troops and equipment as planned at about 1315 but then ran into heavy flak. Several of the aircraft were hit and one ditched into the North Sea. Its crew were picked up by the air sea rescue organisation.

The next day the Wing were airborne again at 1230 hours, this time towing their Waco CG-4A gliders for the first time on operations from Cottesmore. These gliders could carry a payload of 3,900-5,400 lbs, and were used to carry the following:

13 fully armed Glider Infantry plus pilot and co-pilot.

A Jeep and 6 men.

A Jeep trailer and 9 men .

A Bulldozer and 3 men.

A 75mm Howitzer, 18 rounds of ammunition and 5 men.

A 105mm anti-tank gun, ammunition and 5 men.

Miscellaneous cargo, fuel ammunition, rations, medical and evacuate the wounded.

The 82 tugs and gliders headed for Groesbeek, a small town south east of Nijmegen with reinforcements for the hard pressed troops on the ground. The plan was for the gliders to land just south east of Groesbeek at 1540 hours. When they arrived the zone was still in the hands of the German defenders; they had to wait until it was cleared. After the gliders had been released, the tugs ran into heavy flak near the Reichswald Forest and three were shot down. A re-supply mission, on 18 September, had to be cancelled because of bad weather which continued until the 23rd when the wing carried out another glider tow, this time 89 tug and glider combinations carrying reinforcements for the 82nd Airborne Division at Grave.

One aircraft was hit by flak after releasing its glider and caught fire. The crew managed to bring it under control until the aircraft could land at Brussels. Three days later, on 26 September,

A C-109 (a B-24 'Liberator' bomber converted into a fuel tanker) of 36 TCS waits on a frosty Cottesmore airfield in 1945. *(Photo: W Ferguson)*

another maximum effort re-supply mission was flown by the 316th TCG who provided 72 aircraft, carrying guns and ammunition for the British 52nd Airportable Division to an improvised landing strip near Grave. The 82nd Airborne Division had secured the crossing of the Meuse at Grave by the 18th but was having great difficulty in taking the bridge over the Waal which was protected by the heavy fortifications at Nijmegen. With the assistance of the reinforcements flown in, both Nijmegen and the Waal Bridge were taken by the 21st after an attack by the airborne troops supported by tanks of the British Guards Division.

The third and furthest objective, the bridge over the River Rhine at Arnhem, proved to be the most heavily defended of all. The 9th and 10th SS Panzer Divisions faced the airborne troops who were without either armour or artillery and although the 2nd Parachute Battalion held the northern end of the road bridge for four days denying its use to the Panzer reinforcements, by the afternoon of the 20th they were overwhelmed. On the 25th they were ordered to withdraw under cover of darkness to the south. Only 2,400 of the remaining 9,000 men got away.

A pair of Curtiss C-46D's of 36 TCS at Cottesmore in 1945. *(Photo: W Ferguson)*

Anglo-American relations.

Back at Cottesmore the Americans had made many friends with the local people. As well as the 316th TCG personnel, the paratroopers had set up tented camps at Braunstone Park near Leicester and at Ashwell Camp near Oakham with associated services such as a parachute maintenance company, equipment stores and maintenance units. Compared to the local people the Americans were better fed, clothed and generally more affluent, they were also very generous particularly to the local girls and children. They are still remembered for their gifts of candies, gum, ice cream, spam and nylons. One lady remembered as a child being given particularly delicious sweets which rejoiced in the name of Fanny Farmer's Candies. The Americans had their own favourite local haunts, amongst which were the Victoria Hall at Oakham for dances and the Black Horse pub at Langham; in addition, on the base the 316th TCG had their own excellent dance band which played in the Red Cross Club, the American Aero Club and the NAAFI. On entertainment nights, transport would range round the Rutland towns and villages to bring in the local girls. But the gentle arts were not the only activities in the area, the 316th TCG also had a very successful football team known as Berger's Bouncers; there is a record of them playing the Bear Cats of the 9th Service Command on the hallowed turf of the Yorkshire Cricket Club at Headingley, Leeds, in front of a crowd of 40,000 spectators.

By this time the end of the war seemed to be almost in sight and there must have been some temptation for bases so far away from the actual fighting to relax, if only slightly, but there was still time to let slip the odd devastating blow on both sides. The early hours of 4 March 1945 was one such occasion. Lancasters returning to Woolfox Lodge were bounced by intruding German fighters and two were shot down. At 0115 hours Lancaster ND387(K) crashed near Cottesmore, and at 0135 hours Lancaster JB699(T) dived vertically into the ground on Cottesmore airfield killing the entire crew. This operation known to the Luftwaffe as Operation GISELA was designed to destroy the RAF bombers as they came in to land. Twenty-four RAF aircraft were shot down that night by Junkers Ju88 night fighters. The anti-aircraft defences could not shoot at the fighters for fear of hitting the bombers and the bombers were extremely vulnerable with landing gear and flaps down after a long and tiring mission over enemy territory. The intruders pressed home their attacks on Cottesmore itself, dropping 17 bombs, 3 of which failed to explode. There were no casualties but two aircraft and one Waco glider were damaged. Mr Hollis' farm house which was just outside the airfield perimeter was also damaged as was the perimeter track near his farm.

In December 1944, the 316th TCG received the first of seven Consolidated C-109 fuel tankers, allocated for use by its four TC Squadrons. These aircraft were modified B-24 Liberator bombers, whose armour and interior fittings had been replaced with auxiliary fuel tanks, permitting an additional 2,415 gallons of fuel to be carried, increasing their total fuel load to 4,850 gallons. The C-109 had originally been designed to enable fuel to be flown into bases, then unbuilt, in China. These aircraft were flown on the hazardous run "over the Hump" (Himalayas) from India to China, for the initial Boeing B-29 Superfortress long-range operations flown against Japan. Although a few 316th TCG crews were converted to fly these aircraft, little use was made of them as there were no reinforced runways in an advanced area on the continent capable of holding the full weight of the aircraft. (In a test, a fully loaded C-109 landed on the asphalt runway at Brussels, and promptly sank through the surface). Only two missions were flown in C-109s from Cottesmore, both on 11 February, one carrying 1,707 galls of fuel to Achiet in France, but by 8 April 1945 all of these aircraft had been transferred to the 349th TCG at Barkston Heath.

After MARKET the Cottesmore squadrons were kept busy transporting fuel, ammunition and other supplies to airfields near the front line in France, Belgium and Holland, returning with the wounded. During March 1945, a small number of Curtiss C-46D Commando transport aircraft were allocated to the four TC squadrons at Cottesmore, to replace lost and damaged C-47s and C-53s. Slightly larger and wider-bodied than the C-47/C-53, they were capable of carrying 40 (as against 28) fully armed troops, or 10,000 lbs (6,000 lbs) of cargo. Then it was time for Operation VARSITY which was designed to force a crossing of the River Rhine near Wesel, the last natural barrier to the German heartland.

On 21 March the 316th TCG moved out of Cottesmore for this Operation, to operate from a forward base at Wethersfield. On this occasion troops of the British 6th Airborne Division were dropped on DZs just west and north west of Hamminkeln, a small town just east of the Rhine, five miles north of Wesel. The drop, made at 1000 hours on 24 March, was again successful but as the aircraft turned away from the target areas they came under heavy flak and small arms fire which disrupted the formation. Two aircraft went down in flames almost immediately in the Hochwald area near the Rhine, one of the crews managing to parachute to safety. They were picked up and returned to Cottesmore two days later. Four other badly damaged aircraft made emergency landings near Eindhoven, one of them burning out after touch down, though not before the crew were able to scuttle to safety. About half the remainder received flak damage to a greater or lesser degree but were able to return to Cottesmore without serious casualties. Further supply missions were flown deeper into Germany during the remainder of the month and into April. None of the 316th TCG C-46D Commandos were flown on operations, but as a result of losses sustained during VARSITY by the 313th and 349th TCGs, units solely equipped with these aircraft, Cottesmore's Commandos were transferred to those units during April. Then suddenly it was all over.

Peace breaks out!.
At 1500 hours on 8 May the Prime Minister's announcement of the end of the war was broadcast over Cottesmore's 'Tannoy' system. The voice of the Station Commander, Squadron Leader G D F Keddie, followed with an announcement that a Service of Thanksgiving would take place in the Station Church at 1530 hours. The Rector of Ashwell, the Rev P W Rushmer conducted the congregation through the familiar words, LAC Grimley read the lesson and Sgt. Sykes played the organ.

The men of the 316th TCG USAAF, immediately turned their thoughts towards home. On 11 May the first 236 Officers and 1,020 enlisted men briefly lined up like September swallows, then left Cottesmore for good in assorted vehicles. Three days later the first detachments boarded the troopships Santa Paula, Henry Gibbons and Excelsior at Liverpool and headed for New York with the alacrity of men 3 years overseas and in mortal danger for much of that time. Arriving to a hero's welcome on 24 May, they moved onto Camp Kilmer in New Jersey and then home. The C-47 and C-53 crews flew towards the setting sun and Pope Field, North Carolina with scarcely a backward glance.

Thus ended the first occupation of Cottesmore by friendly foreign forces and for three months afterwards nothing was heard in Rutland but the gentle sobbing of the girls they left behind them. Or so we have been told!

The memorial stone laid by the Americans outside the Station Headquarters

CHAPTER THREE

The early post-war years - the RAF returns!

On 6 August 1945 an awed USAAF Major Tibbet eased his B-29 'Enola Gay' back from Hiroshima towards his Pacific Island base with a rapidly rising radioactive cloud behind him. Three days later another atomic bomb was dropped on Nagasaki. The Atomic Age had begun. On 14 August World War 2 was over. There was a short pause for some slightly uneasy rejoicing; at Cottesmore the unit history laconically noted: 15 August VJ Day, the celebration of victory over Japan was observed by all ranks in a fitting manner, skeleton staffs being worked over the two day standdown.

After the Americans left Cottesmore the station was officially transferred from the IXth TCC Substitution Unit to 7 Group on 1 July. A bronze memorial plaque presented by the USAAF stands in front of Cottesmore Station Headquarters catching the eyes of the countless Orderly Officers and Orderly Sergeants raising and lowering the RAF Ensign during their tour of duty. It is singularly apposite to Cottesmore, no less now than when placed there so many years ago. It reads: 'May the memory of comradeship sown in the skies of Europe forever be as green as the fields of Cottesmore'.

1668 Heavy Conversion Unit,

The Station was prepared for the arrival of 1668 Heavy Conversion Unit (HCU) from RAF Bottesford, in the Vale of Belvoir, as 5015 Squadron Detachment were working on the repair of runways, station buildings and the demolition of defence works. This unit had the distinction of bringing three of the most famous RAF aircraft of the war to Cottesmore, the Spitfire, Mosquito and Lancaster. Enough has been written about them elsewhere to take up space here, but that fine aircraft the Beaufighter, which also came, was one of the few to have the distinction of having verse written about it by Gavin Ewart:

> When a Beau goes in,
> Into the drink,
> It makes you think,
> Because, you see, they always sink.
> But nobody says 'Poor lad',
> Or goes about looking sad,
> Because, you see, it's war,
> It's the unalterable law.
>
> You shouldn't cry,
> Or say a prayer or sigh.
> In the cold sea in the dark,
> It isn't a lark.
> But it isn't original sin
> It's just a Beau going in.

The bulk of the personnel at Bottesford including students and ground equipment moved to Cottesmore by road in MT supplied by 7 Group on 15, 16 and 17 September; some 30 aircraft flew in at intervals afterwards. As a consequence the station strength rose rapidly with quite a high proportion of Women's Auxiliary Air Force personnel. As the September 1945 medical report succinctly put it:

a. Health of station   Good
b. Number of epidemics   Nil

c.	Number of casualties	Nil
d.	Number of crashes	Nil
e.	Number of VD cases	5
f.	Station is overcrowded	

The problem was quickly solved by the rapid demobilisation from all ranks. By January 1946 numbers had fallen to 1,260 although flying training continued with a new course of eight crews every two weeks. The overall strength of the RAF was also in headlong decline from a peak of 9,200 aircraft and 1,079,836 personnel in May 1945 to a little over 1,000 aircraft and 38,000 personnel.

Lancaster and crew of 1668 Heavy Conversion Unit at Cottesmore circa August 1945.
(Photo: Garbett and Golding Collection via J. Kilburn)

Group Excercises

Part of the flying training included weekly Group controlled exercises, sometimes flown by day, sometimes by night. An example of one of these, Exercise ERIC, took place on 1 October 1945 when 7 Group tasked North Luffenham, Cottesmore, Swinderby and Finningley to provide Lancasters for a route from those bases to St.Abbs Head and a rendezous at 57 North 001 East, to Aberdeen, to the Farne Islands near Bamburgh, to Hucknall, to a finishing point at Norwich, to Hunstanton, to Friskney to Bases. From the RV the aircraft were tasked to fly in a 'gaggle'. They were escorted by Mustangs of 12 Group to beat off expected attacks from attacking fighters. In this exercise, camera guns were fitted and photographs taken of the target rather than practice bombs dropped. Two days after this exercise a crew was lost on the pilot's initial night solo when Lancaster NG274 flown by Flight Lieutenant Baker lost an engine. His approach to the airfield on three engines appeared to onlookers to be normal if not completely lined up with the runway. The pilot apparently decided to go round again as he passed over the lights. The aircraft appeared initially to gain height as it flew over the airfield but 50 seconds later a sheet of flame was seen in line with the runway.

The following week's Exercise was a 'BULLSEYE' in which the same station's aircraft as the

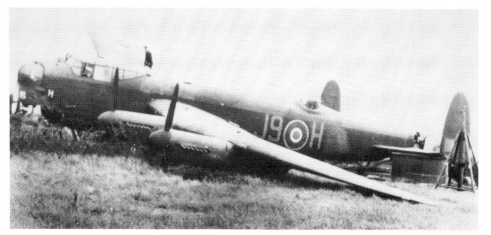

A Lancaster of 1668 Heavy Conversion Unit after a mishap. *(Photo: N Franklin)*

previous week were joined by other Lancasters flying between 15,500 and 19,000 feet, Wellingtons between 14,500 and 15,000 and Mosquitos between 20,000 and 21,500 feet. This was a night exercise which took them out over France before turning back over the bombing range at Otmoor near Oxford where practice bombs were dropped. The target was marked by Target Indicators dropped by aircraft from 8 Group, fighters were encountered all along the route and 'window' was dropped by the bombers. The order was completed by an instruction to the gunners to maintain a good search throughout and to flash their lights at the fighters immediately they had brought their guns to bear and in a position to open fire

With station numbers rapidly declining and the weather unusually foul there were lots of restrictions on flying that winter, nevertheless 57 crews had been trained by 7 March 1946 when 1668 HCU disbanded.

Woolfox Lodge's career as a flying station had, to all intents and purposes, already come to an end in August 1945 when 1654 HCU with its Lancasters was disbanded. It was however later used as a relief landing ground for Cottesmore aircraft, as a Maintenance Unit and as a Bloodhound SAM site. At North Luffenham 1653 HCU with Stirlings, Lancasters, Spitfires, Hurricanes, Beaufighters and Mosquitos continued until October 1946.

1668 HCU was replaced at Cottesmore by 16 OTU which arrived on 22 March 1946 from Upper Heyford, equipped with 4 Oxfords and 15 Mosquito T IIIs and B XVI aircraft.

The Mosquito had been planned as a private venture by de Havilland as a small, light aircraft with no defensive armament, relying entirely on speed for defence. It was received with indifference in official circles! But primarily due to the interest of Sir Wilfred Freeman on the Air Council, de Havillands were, at last authorised to proceed with a limited production on 29 December 1939. The first prototype Mosquito made its maiden flight from Hatfield only 11 months later, on 25 November 1940, and amazed the onlookers by performing upward rolls with one propellor feathered and attaining a level speed of almost 400 mph. It became the fastest aircraft in the RAF from September 1941 until early 1944 and the fastest RAF bomber until the Canberra jet was introduced in 1951.

When it joined the squadrons its speed was at first utilised as a reconnaissance aircraft. On 20 September 1941 it flew a daylight reconaissance sortie at 23,000 feet over Brest, La Pallice, Bordeaux and Paris and although it was chased by three Bf 109 fighters, they were unable to catch it; a state of affairs which gave enormous satisfaction to the crew. This versatile aircraft also flew as a night fighter, a day and night bomber, a pathfinder, a rocket equipped ground attack aircraft and a Coastal Command

Mosquito T.Mk.III trainers of 16 OTU in front of the Cottesmore Signals Square. GA-F is RR292. *(Photo: Chaz Bowyer).*

anti shipping aircraft carrying 8 x 60 pound rockets which when fired as a salvo were equivalent to a broadside from a 10,000 ton cruiser.

The Mosquito proved uniquely effective as a pathfinder aircraft, a task for which it was equipped with 'Oboe', a radar aid which enabled aircraft to find a target accurately through cloud or haze, although the actual marking was done visually using a shallow dive technique. In the high level bomber role their loss rate dropped to one per 2,000 sorties, a Bomber Command record. This strategic role was however less appealing to the public than several remarkable low level precision attacks which might have appeared in the 'Boy's Own Book of Daring Escapades'. One of these was the raid on Amiens Prison by 19 Mosquitos led by Group Captain P C Pickard on 18 February 1944. They attacked at rooftop height and breached the prison walls, allowing 258 prisoners to escape. The leader, who had lingered to control the attack, was shot down by Focke-Wulf 190s, probably the only aircraft able to catch them at that time.

By the late summer of 1944 another aircraft appeared on the scene which radically altered the Mosquito's relatively sanguine situation. A photo reconnaissance Mosquito of 60 Squadron was flying over Southern Germany where they had had much their own way for some months, operating alone and unarmed. Suddenly they sighted the condensation trails of an unidentified aircraft. They set off after it, but it lost height, gained speed and easily evaded them. A few moments later as the Mosquito was approaching Gunzburg-Leipheim airfield at 22,000 feet, one of the escorting Mustangs warned of an approaching aircraft rapidly closing in on him from astern. Coming in at high speed, the aircraft opened fire at a range of 900 metres. Still firing but without scoring any hits, the graceful, grey Me 262 jet overshot and the escorting Mustangs tried to turn into it. They could not complete more than a 90 degree turn before it flashed past them. After attempting to complete his photographic run over the airfield, the escort leader again warned: 'Break right'. The Me 262, firing all the time began to turn into the formation. It overshot at a TAS of about 850 km/hr, then went into a majestic climbing turn to starboard. The Mustangs and the Mosquito chased after it but were easily outpaced. Things had changed.

Mosquitos were quite a handful for inexperienced pilots at take off and landing as the accident record at Cottesmore testified. Thirteen were written off in accidents within two years; but with flying reaching 500 hours per month, the rate was not considered serious for a training unit. On 21 December 1945, Cottesmore was transferred from 7 Group to 91 Group Bomber Command and although 16 OTU continued to train Bomber Command crews they also trained 48 pilots and 30 navigators of the French

Mosquito FB.Mk.VI of 204 AFS *(Photo: R Sturtivant)*

Air Force. The winter of 1946/47 was another bitter one all over Europe. Severe blizzards throughout February prevented a single aircraft from leaving the ground. Cottesmore was cut off for a while in March 1947, and a Lancaster from Lindholme had to drop bread and medical supplies onto the airfield. It was still snowing in May, and on 16 May Mosquito RV363, whilst landing too fast in poor visibility, overran the runway onto soft ground and overturned.

With the arrival of Spring came a change in the training syllabus. All bombing training stopped and the course aimed instead at a simple conversion onto type. With shortages in manning in many support sections, notably Air Traffic Control as people were demobilised in increasing numbers, training became of necessity a more leisurely affair and an intermediate stage was introduced. When aircrew had completed their training to 'wings' standard they went onto Advanced Flying Schools before going onto Operational Training Units. 16 OTU was re-named 204 Advanced Flying School (AFS) on 1 May 1947, and the station changed its Group once again, this time to 21 Group, Flying Training Command, and its Mosquito B XVIs were exchanged for FB VIs.

Changes in policy, organisation and administration were rapid in these early post war years when the newly won peace occasionally looked threatened as when the veneer of cooperation between the wartime allies - always fragile - finally ruptured and in Churchill's phrase: 'From Stettin on the Baltic to Trieste on the Adriatic an iron curtain descended across the continent'. But there were encouraging signs too; the signing of the Charter of the United Nations by 46 countries for example; unfortunately the five permanent members of the Security Council were given a veto which Russia

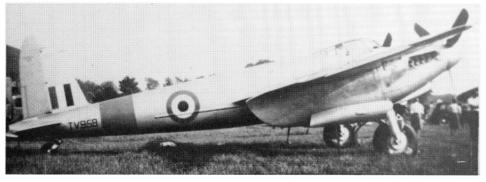

All silver with yellow training bands adorn this T.Mk.III Mosquito, previously of 204 AFS, but shown here with Home Command Examining Wing *(Photo: via G. Cruikshank)*

used 77 times in the first 10 years of the UNs existance. The first real hint of European cooperation came when Holland, Belgium and Luxembourg cooperated economically in the Benelux Union.

At Cottesmore, Commanding Officers were changing with a bewildering rapidity: Group Captain J H T Simpson DSO from September 1945 - December 1945, Group Captain H McC White December 1945 - March 1946, Group Captain R A A Cole CBE March 1946 - May 1946, Group Captain N W F Mason May 1946 - February 1947 and finally some stability with Group Captain A H S Lucas who remained for 3 years until February 1950.

The AFS had an unfortunate end to its time at Cottesmore with the loss of two Mosquitos and their crews within four days. On 6 February Flying Officer Goodchild and Flight Lieutenant J R Spencer were seen to take off normally, if a little more steeply than ideal, only to crash shortly afterwards. On 9 February Flying Officer Robinson crashed only 500 yards from the end of the runway. The aircraft was burning furiously when the Fire Section arrived and they were unable to save the crew. 204 AFS left Cottesmore for Driffield on 1 March 1948.

7 Flying Training School

If you ask the young men from any nation who pass through Cottesmore why they joined their Air Force, you would get none of the jingoism that sometimes appears in the headlines of tabloid newspapers; there would be little boisterous bandying about of words like duty, honour, glory, might, majesty, dominion, power etc. Most would simply say that they joined for the fun of learning to fly; but what really turned on the dashing young man was an open cockpit, the wind in the hair, in the struts, the wires, the scarf blowing in the slipstream, the 'sha sha sha' of an idling propellor, the smell of oil and petrol in the nostrils, the crushed insects on the windscreen and the sporty sideslip onto a grass strip, preferably with an equally sporting young woman looking on. Ah, those were the days! The young lads at Cottesmore in 1948 would have known; they had de Havilland Tiger Moths to play with.

The Tiger Moth was the last biplane and the last aircraft with a permanently open cockpit to fly with the RAF. It had a pretty little 130 hp de Havilland Gypsy Major engine that gave it a cruising speed of 93 mph and was introduced to service in February 1932. Over 4,200 were built in Britain, mostly by Morris Motors of Cowley. A further 2,949 were built in Australia, Canada and New Zealand and it became the standard abinitio trainer of the RAF throughout the war and for some considerable time after. It came to Cottesmore with 7 Flying Training School (FTS) from Kirton-in-Lindsey on 16 March 1948.

Pilots who flew Tiger Moths look back to them with immense nostalgia, particularly if, like Squadron Leader Jim Willis, who ended a long and distinguished career in the RAF as an Ops Officer at

A 7FTS DH82 Tiger Moth about to lift off from Cottesmore *(Photo:MoD)*

Cottesmore in 1989, you learned to fly them in Rhodesia (now Zimbabwe) in 1952. You must have heard stories about being on top of a loop with nothing on the clock when the engine stops - a trick of which the Tiger Moth was capable and quite willing to demonstrate. It is a moment which concentrates the mind of all pilots wonderfully in any aircraft - but in the Tiger Moth it had other repercussions. You see, it had no self starter, no comforting cartridge to get you going again. The engine was started by swinging the propeller. In the event of it stopping in the air, you needed a bit of airspace and a modicum of speed for the wind to spin the prop for you. In addition to small details like this, no brakes, no radio, a tail wheel undercarriage, only the most basic of instruments were considered necessary. You see the charm of it? With their narrow track undercarriages and butterfly light wings, the Tiger Moth could be tricky on the ground in all but the lightest of winds, and so young trainee pilots really did learn to fly by the seat of their pants.

Students graduated from the Tiger Moth to the North American Harvard - another classic and much loved training aircraft. Most pilots recall the space in the cockpit, the big radial 550hp Pratt and Whitney Wasp engine and the swing on take-off; most groundcrew remember it for the extraordinary rasping noise made by the engine, caused by its direct drive propellor with very high tip speeds. It was

7FTS Harvard at Cottesmore in 1952
(Photo: Wg Cdr. E Stephenson)

one of the first American aircraft ever ordered for the RAF who received the first batch of 200 in June 1939. From its first appearance in Britain with 3 FTS at Grantham until it was replaced at Cottesmore in 1952 by the Boulton Paul Balliol, its rasp was as familiar to the villagers of Rutland as the morning song of the blackbird or the sound of falling rain.

7 FTS was responsible for training pilots for the RAF and the Royal Navy; it also carried out refresher courses and instrument rating courses. No officer training was given and student pilots had

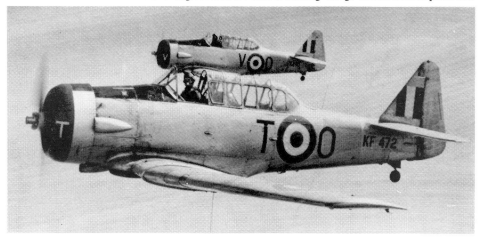
A nice picture of a pair of 7FTS Harvards circa 1952 *(Photo: G Hallion)*

little or no status with the rank of cadet pilot. When they graduated they were promoted to the rank of Pilot 4 from where they were promoted successively to Pilot 1 and ultimately Master Pilot. The system was not terribly popular and only lasted until 1950 when cadets who were selected for commissions on graduation were posted to Officer Cadet Training Units. There was a further change in the status of the student pilots during 1950 when they were called Officer Cadets during training and commissioned on graduation.

In Europe the 'Cold War' was dividing the continent into uneasy blocks. The Americans offered generous economic help to any country that requested it under a plan devised by the American Secretary of State, General George Marshall, and the British, French and Americans jointly proposed the fusion of their three occupied zones in 1948 to become the Federal Republic of West Germany in a move to stimulate the shattered economy. This idea was received by the Russians with the utmost suspicion and on 23 June 1948 the Soviet authorities stopped all land traffic into and out of the Western sector of Berlin. The two million people who had survived there had suffered greatly over the past months, and they were now to undergo even more tribulations as the Western nations were faced with the problem of supplying them with the 4,000 tons of materials they required daily in order to survive. The solution became known as the Berlin Air Lift.

Cottesmore's Rutland neighbour, 240 Operational Conversion Unit at North Luffenham was equipped at the time with Dakotas, Vickers Valettas, de Havilland Devons and Ansons and was called upon to help. Its Dakotas joined the air armada flying the lifeline along the corridor into the beleaguered city. At the height of the air-lift, one day in April, 1,383 aircraft arrived at 62 second intervals carrying 13,215 tons of material. The Russians finally gave in to this resolute action and at one minute past midnight on 12 May 1949 they lifted the blockade.

This flurry of activity in Europe caused the momentum of training at Cottesmore to be increased from some 700 flying hours per month to 2,675 by mid 1950. With inexperienced pilots and relatively old single-engined aircraft the school had its share of accidents: generally heavy landings, pilots forgetting to select undercarriage down or problems with the swing on take off in the case of the Harvard, ground loops in the case of the Tiger Moth (an aircraft with a particular aversion to cross winds) but there was no doubt that, as a proportion of hours flown, serious accidents were becoming fewer. With lower landing speeds the chances of carrying out survivable crash landings increased, even if some of them were spectacular like the one in July when a Harvard lost its engine and crash landed near Asfordby. The wings were torn off as it passed through a hedge and the fuselage came to rest in a vertical position. Happily the pilot crawled out and was helped to safety by a Mr John Parlby who had witnessed the arrival with some alarm.

The passing out parade of Number 9 (Pilot's) Course on 2 June 1949 had more than the usual significance for 7 FTS and for Cottesmore as a whole. The Lord Lieutenant of Rutland, The Earl of Ancaster, presented 'Wings' to graduate students, the Unit with it's 7 FTS Badge and Cottesmore with it's Station Badge. The Station Badge contains a hunting horn and a 5 pointed American star superimposed on an inverted horseshoe to symbolise the station's affinity with the Cottesmore (fox) Hunt and to recall the American wartime occupation of the base. The motto, 'We rise to our obstacles', is intended to convey the station's spirit but with an obvious hunting theme. The Cottesmore hounds were established at Exton (a mere stone's throw from the airfield) in 1732 but moved to Cottesmore village in 1788. They are now kennelled just outside Oakham and have enjoyed a close association for most of RAF Cottesmore's existence.

World events, not unnaturally, continued to influence the increasing numbers of pilots arriving for training at Cottesmore. The polarisation of east and west led to the formation of NATO and the Warsaw Pact, the production by Russia of its own atomic bomb and then on 25 June 1950 Communist North Korea crossed the border into South Korea in what the President of the United States, Mr Truman, called 'raw unprovoked aggression'. There was an immediate resolution of protest in the

Security Council of the United Nations which resulted in the United Nation's first commitment to military action. This was possible because the Russians were boycotting the Security Council at the time and so the Soviet Representative was not present to register a veto. The bulk of the forces opposing the Communist attack were American and South Korean but British and Commonwealth forces were also committed, and jet propelled fighters were employed by both sides in large numbers for the first time.

All British young men were required to do two years National Service and the Korean situation prompted many of these to be taken on as aircrew, so the organisation of 7 FTS was changed to facilitate the extra numbers passing through. Flying Wing now had one Percival Prentice squadron, two Harvard squadrons and a Headquarters squadron; the latter to maintain a flow of instructors, to give instrument rating tests and to act as a sort of standardisation squadron. The increasing numbers also created problems of accommodation and administration, which was overcome by the construction of a Number 2 Officers' Mess, opened in March 1951. Most of the students were accommodated in comfortable, if noisy, pre-fabricated buildings on the sports field to the south of the permanent Officers' Mess.

With more accommodation, more instructors and more aircraft the Cottesmore circuit became frantic. Anything up to 18 aircraft at a time in the visual circuit, others joining after cross country exercises and others on radar circuits created immense problems for Air Traffic Control; the noise upset the local villagers (the Harvard in particular was no pussyfoot) and there was a very real risk to flight safety. Various measures were tried to overcome the difficulty including a system of dual runways. It did not work. The final solution, and one which was reasonably successful, was for the Prentices to overflow into the Spitalgate circuit just south of Grantham and the Harvards to Woolfox Lodge.

The Prentice had several advantages over the Tiger Moth which it replaced, but it also posed more complications to the young trainee pilots. It had a more powerful engine with an enclosed cockpit and side by side seating for instructor and student (the first RAF basic trainer to have this arrangement). It also had a variable pitch airscrew, flaps and a radio and could operate in 'all weathers'.

University student training.

In June 1951 the HQ Squadron was given the additional task of training university cadets to 'Wings' standard, which they planned to reach after about 70 hours. In 1952 a further task of providing acclimatisation training for Rhodesian and Canadian trained pilots was added but even this wasn't all; records show many other nationalities appearing in the course lists including Burmese and so the

Percival Prentice of 7FTS. *(Photo: via G Cruikshank).*

53

intensity of flying continued to increase such that in February 1952 in one 28 day period the monthly task of 3,143 hours was exceeded by 422 hours. From this point the system was changed to give the students the rank of Acting Pilot Officer after successfully completing their Initial Training School.

The Cottesmore cosmopolitan tradition was continuing with instructors as well as students. The February 1952 ORB compiled by Squadron Leader H E White DFC AFC recorded: Seven Qualified Flying Instructors (QFIs) were posted in during the month including a Canadian, four South Africans and a Rhodesian. The Wing now has three Canadians, four South Africans, one Rhodesian, one American, one Frenchman and 'some Englishmen'.

One flying incident, which resulted in a near miss, illustrated an everyday problem: an inexperienced young man was flying in a Prentice when cloud built up very quickly. In the mistaken belief that he was not to fly below 2,000 feet, he remained at this height and flew into cloud although he had not been taught any instrument flying. The experience made him feel sick. He said that he remembered little more till he broke cloud near the circuit, made a hasty approach and ran off the runway after landing. 'He was taken to Sick Quarters' remarks Squadron Leader White (his moustache bristling), 'and injected with some common sense.'

An unusual night incident occurred after the airfield had closed one evening when a Harvard, piloted by an FTS instructor from Moreton in the Marsh, landed at Cottesmore without the aid of runway lighting. The aircraft electrics had failed and the weather at Moreton in the Marsh had deteriorated. The pilot flew north east to reach better flying weather, saw Cottesmore's pundit (the identification light flashing CM) and orbitted it until he could see the runway in the moonlight. He made his approach and landed safely. The Station Duty Officer had not switched on the Drem lighting (as he would normally have done outside working hours in an emergency) because the aircraft had been unable to signal its approach.

As part of the continuing campaign for the support of the local people, Group Captain D J Alvey OBE, the Station Commander, visited Oakham Urban District Council to present a copy of the

Major B. B. Tolland USAF, Officer Commanding 2 Sqn 7FTS in 1952. The Harvard carries his own personal yellow and black markings on cowling and wheel hubs. *(Photo: G Hallion)*

Station Badge which had been manufactured on the unit. In his presentation speech he stressed the need for the Council and his Unit to keep in close touch, he wanted the association to be more than mere cooperation. He asked the Council to look on Cottesmore as a local industry producing pilots for the service of the country, the good wishes and encouragement of the local people being a most important factor. Other events that year which involved the active participation of local organisations were an Escape and Evasion exercise in June and a Battle of Britain 'At Home' day in September.

The Battle of Britain At Home day on 20 September 1952 was slightly disappointing in that only about 2,900 visitors came to watch the flying display and side shows etc. This was almost certainly due to the counter attraction provided by an Open Day at nearby North Luffenham, then the home of the Canadair Sabres of No 1(F) Wing, Royal Canadian Air Force.

Group Captain R Sorel-Cameron CBE AFC took over the station from Group Captain Alvey on 3 October 1952. The graduation parade that month was for No 91 (P) Course and was commanded by Major B B Toland USAF, OC the Squadron from which the course had graduated, and was reviewed by Air Marshal R L R Atcherley AOC 12 Group. He was a legendary figure in the RAF (generally known at 'Batchy'), one of two easily confused twin brothers who inspired many stories which survived long after they had retired.

Arrival of the Balliol

A fine 'line abreast' formation of 7FTS Balliols in 1953. *(Photo: Aeroplane)*

During 1947, the Air Ministry had laid down the specification for a new advanced trainer. The specification was changed several times by the Air Ministry, originally being designed as a three-seat advanced trainer powered by an early turboprop engine, the Armstrong Siddeley Mamba. Finally, the specification was changed to a two-seat piston-engined trainer powered by a Rolls-Royce Merlin 35 engine.

Boulton Paul were one of the companies vying for the contract, and their first Merlin powered prototype, now designated the Balliol T2, was first flown on 10 July 1948. Seventeen pre-production aircraft were then ordered for extended Service trials with a view to adopting the type as a replacement for the well-proven Harvard. One of these, VR598, was issued to 7 FTS for a two month trial period on 9 June 1950, followed later by a further three in February 1952 for an extended period. After the initial trials, large contracts had been placed for the Balliol, but these were cut back in 1951, when further changes in flying training policy favoured the introduction of a jet type for advanced instruction. As a result the Balliol was to form the equipment of only one FTS, No 7, although it later served at the RAF College, Cranwell, until superseded by the Vampire T11 in 1956.

A Balliol of 7FTS above solid cloud on 5 December 1952 *(Photo: MoD)*

7 FTS started receiving small numbers of production Balliol T2s from the middle of August 1952 to replace its Harvards. In January 1953, 16 aircraft were received directly from the Boulton Paul factory in Wolverhampton, and to make room for them a further 10 Harvards were despatched from the unit. By the end of March 1953 the changeover was complete.

The power available (1,245hp) came in handy on more than one occasion, for example in September 1952 when an instructor and student were overshooting from a practice forced landing; the student raised the flaps and the aircraft sank dangerously; a fistful of power applied by the instructor averted a potentially nasty incident. The first two major accidents to the new aircraft were recorded during January 1953: the first aircraft was written off by an inexperienced pilot trying unsuccessfully to recover from a bad landing, the second occured when Acting Pilot Officer M C C Courcy was killed when his aircraft, which had been seen carrying out low-level aerobatic manoeuvres, failed to recover from one before hitting the ground at Borderville Farm near Stamford.

7FTS Instructors pose in front of a Balliol in 1953. Wing Commander George McKenzie is in the centre front row. *(Photo: Wg Cdr E. Stephenson)*

On 15 July 1953, the Queen reviewed the Royal Air Force at Odiham as part of the Coronation Ceremonies. Aircraft from all Commands were drawn up in a vast static display on the airfield while overhead one of the biggest formations of aircraft seen for many years flew past in salute. Twelve Balliols from Cottesmore formed a small part of that flypast.

1953 was also the last full year of 7 FTS's association with Cottesmore. During the latter part, as changing defence requirements were made known, it was decided that the Unit would be disbanded in March 1954. In fact during the final departure parade, the reviewing officer Air Marshal L F Pendred, C-in-C Flying Training Command, announced that 7 FTS would live on at Valley, Anglesey, with 202 AFS being immediately redesignated 7 FTS, operating Vampire FB5s and T11s. During its stay at Cottesmore, from 16 March 1948 until 24 March 1954 the unit had successfully trained nearly 1,000 RAF students in addition to all the other post graduate students from all over the world.

With clouds of snow streaming out behind, Boulton Paul Balliol WG131 gets airborne from a very wintry Cottesmore in 1954. *(Photo: Wg Cdr E. Stephenson)*

CHAPTER FOUR

The first jet bomber.

Canberra B2's of 149 Squadron *(Photo: A. S. Thomas)*

The aircraft that replaced the trainers of 7 FTS at Cottesmore became one of the most successful and certainly the most durable of all RAF aircraft. The English Electric Canberra was the first jet bomber to be produced in Britain and the first to serve in the RAF. Built in the tradition of the Mosquito, it was unarmed and relied on speed, altitude and manoeuvrability to escape fighters and for many years after its introduction it did this with almost insolent ease. It was originally proposed for radar bombing only with a crew of two, but very early in production (from the 5th prototype) the specification was changed to B2 standard with a three man crew and a visual bomb aiming position in the nose as well as the radar bombing capability.

It was with this mark of Canberra that 3 Group Canberras of 15, 44, 57 and 149 squadrons flew into Cottesmore from Coningsby in May 1954. The aircraft had already proved itself with several epic flights. 12 Squadron Canberras had carried out a 24,000 mile flight to the Caribbean and Latin America in November 1952. An RAF Flying College B2 from Manby, "Aries 4", broke the London to Cape Town record in December 1953, a distance of 6,009 miles at an average speed of 486.6 mph. Normal cruising speed was .72 Mach (about 410 knots) at heights up to 50,000 feet. A total of 1,461 were built including the Martin B-57 version which was built under licence in America. The Canberra was first flown at Warton on 13 May 1949 by Roland Beamont, and gives every indication at the moment that it will continue in RAF service well into the 1990s.

Due to the contraction of the RAF at the end of WWII many units were disbanded, including many famous squadrons holding distinguished records from the two world wars. In view of the tradition and history associated with these squadrons it was agreed to reduce them to "number only" basis, thus preserving their number plates for future use. In February 1949, an Air Ministry Order stated that it had been decided to resuscitate certain of these squadron number plates by linking them with certain existing front-line squadrons of similar roles and histories. Thus 76 Squadron was linked with 7 Squadron. In the new titles of "linked" squadrons, the number of the existing front-line squadron appeared first, followed by that of the inactive squadron ie 7/76 Squadron. For most of the squadrons affected the links were transitory, for the second numbers in some links were withdrawn to form new squadrons as expansion took place. The linking system has since elapsed, but on 1 February 1949, 44 Squadron became linked with 55 Squadron, until 14 July 1957, so throughout 44 Squadron's tenure at Cottesmore, its correct title was 44/55 Squadron. 15 Squadron had similarly been linked with 21 Squadron during the period 1 February 1949 until 20 September 1953, prior to its move to Cottesmore.

Officer Commanding 15 Squadron's Canberra B2 at Blackbushe in September 1954.
(Photo: via G Cruikshank).

Despite the Canberra's immediate success, certain problems came to light which had to be overcome. There were 128 major accidents to the aircraft between January 1952 and April 1956 (RAF Accident Revue). They were mainly due to runaway tail trim actuators, engine compressor stalls and failures in the undercarriage hydraulic system. It was a slight (though by no means unique) disadvantage that there were no dual trainers until the first T4 arrived in late 1953 after more than two thirds of the Canberras had entered service. In practice, the first generation Canberra pilots did their jet conversion on Gloster Meteors. The QFI would then demonstrate a circuit or two in the Canberra with the student pilot an interested observer from the Rumbold seat, and the navigator trying to give the impression of total nonchalance in the back. The instructor would then get out and leave the fledgling crew to get on with it.

Most crews had early experience of engine compressor stalls which usually seemed to occur at low speeds in slightly nose up attitudes during the last stages of an approach. The sudden 'whirrrrr' of the Rolls-Royce Avon engine in this condition had an electrifying effect on them occurring as it often did on dark and dirty nights on weather diversions to unfamiliar airfields.

The Canberra and its engine were such enormous technological advances over previous bombers and jet engines in the RAF that such problems were almost inevitable. The Avon utilised the first axial flow compressor which replaced the well proven centrifugal compressor giving the engine more power but making it infinitely more complex. It took many years to perfect, and for a time, blighted the life and career of Stanley Hooker, the great Rolls-Royce engineer who led the team that developed it. He explained the phenomenon of compressor stalling in the early Avons in his autobiography: 'Not Much of an Engineer':

'When the pressure ratio is small, at low speed, during starting and acceleration, the inlet and outlet areas are completely out of balance and the air taken in at the front cannot get out at the back. The direction of the airflow through the compressor reverses itself and flows

59

backwards. This causes the blades at the front of the compressor to stall, vibrate and sometimes to snap off.

Most crews recognised the symptoms promptly and the pilots quickly closed the offending engine down and landed as soon as possible. When the bugs were ironed out of the Avon, it became the most important aero engine of the 50s and went on to power the de Havilland Sea Vixen, Hawker Hunter, Vickers Valiant, English Electric Lightning, de Havilland Comet and the Sud-Aviation Caravelle.

Tail trim actuator faults were more catastrophic and were not recognised for some time until a crew baled out and told their tale. This problem was solved after the aircraft was grounded for several months in 1956.

Training and still more training...
Day to day life on these peacetime front line squadrons at Cottesmore was one of constant training and frequent Group and Command exercises when much of the Canberra force was deployed on simulated attacks on targets in the UK and on the Continent. Most of these entailed large numbers of aircraft passing through the target in a very short time using a bombing system called G-H. This was similar to the old Oboe but with a greater range and capable of being used by up to 100 aircraft at the same time. It utilised another function of the GEE box and involved using two transmitter stations, flying along one curved radar line and using the other to set up two warning points. Part of the equipment included a clockwork timing box called a Mouse. The system was very accurate providing that the navigator had set up accurate co-ordinates. He took very great care to do so but it was always a relief to hear the range call 'bomb plotted' especially at night and from high level when there were no checking references.

The Cottesmore Wing also had the facility for visual bomb aiming from the nose of the aircraft using a modified version of the Mark XIV Bombsight. There was very little room to move in the Canberra and in order to get into the nose of the aircraft, the navigator who normally sat in curtained darkness behind the pilot, had to slide supine beneath the GEE box, haul himself upright beside the pilot and then lie prone in the nose. Accurate visual bombing was no easy matter at height, the vision was limited and the aircraft had a maddening habit of swinging back to near the original heading after a correction. One had to make much coarser corrections than one would have expected. It seemed a retrograde step to navigators who had come from an aircraft like the Avro Lincoln where the bomb aimer had a wonderful all round field of view, was able to sit upright in a comfortable soft seat and had an aircraft round him which seemed rock steady, if one did not take account of the difference in performance. With practice however, visual bombing improved.

Navigators relied primarily on GEE, an excellent radar aid provided the flight was over, or near to, the United Kingdom. There was an Air Position Indicator (API) into which was fed true heading from the compass and True Air Speed thus giving the aircraft's position in still air. A few aircraft had radio compasses from which not only radio position lines could be obtained but also CONSOL position lines from Bush Mills in Northern Ireland, Ploneis in Brittany and Stavangar in Norway; very useful on longer flights. In addition range position lines could be taken from UK airfields operating Rebecca homing equipment and true bearings obtained by the pilot - providing there was no objection to breaking radio silence. There was also some flirtation with astro navigation using a hand held sextant, but this was very much a secondary aid requiring laborious movement about the constricted aircraft to the Rumbold seat beside the pilot and without a periscopic sextant, results were far from accurate. A homing and approach aid known as Rebecca and BABS completed the navigators armoury. Training led through a series of stages: unclassified, combat, combat star and select. The more highly classified the crews, the higher they were cleared to drop bombs and the further afield they were authorised to fly. The unit diary for June 1954 records that three crews from 149 Squadron were the first in the Group to be cleared to bomb from 40,000 feet using G-H.

A 57 Squadron Canberra B2 at Cottesmore in 1954 *(Photo: J.J. Halley)*

The Canberra squadrons were not destined for a long stay at Cottesmore. 149 Squadron was the first to go on 24 August 1954 to Ahlhorn in Germany to become the first Canberra squadron in the 2nd Tactical Air Force. The others continued for a while gaining in confidence and expertise and with many more crews reaching high categories. Once they had reached Combat Star category, they became eligible for 'Lone Ranger' overseas flights. In December Flight Lieutenant Gledhill of 15 Squadron flew to Gibraltar, in January Flying Officer Dyson of 15 Squadron and Flight Lieutenant Veale of 44 Squadron to Idris in Libya. These Lone Rangers slowly built up to include flights to Wunsdorf, Wildenrath, Ahlhorn, Gutersloh, Fassburg and Celle in Germany, to Habbaniya in Iraq, El Adem (Libya) Amman (Jordan), Eastleigh (Kenya), Luqa (Malta), Fayid and Abu Sueir (Egypt) and Aden as well as 'Polar Bear' flights to Norway usually landing at Stavangar Sola or Gardermoen near Oslo. Crews were required to have the appropriate capability in the turnround, post and pre flight servicing in the various locations and climates, and were unsupported, although control and command was exercised by Group Headquarters.

In November 1954 six 57 Squadron Canberras flew an 8,000 mile tour of the Middle East under the command of Squadron Leader Ivor Broom DSO DFC (later Air Marshal Sir Ivor Broom). The tour included Baghdad (Iraq), Tripolitania and Amman where King Hussein of Jordan flew a sortie in one of the aircraft.

During February 1955, the three remaining squadrons departed for Honington and Cottesmore was prepared for its next aircraft. During its brief stay the Canberra had attracted the attention of several foreign air forces, notably from South America, and a party of 28 officers and senior NCOs of the Venezuelan Air Force had spent a month at Cottesmore studying the aircraft. This resulted in sales of the aircraft to that country. Many other countries eventually bought it including West Germany, Sweden, Zimbabwe, South Africa, Ecuador, France, Chile, Ethiopia, Peru, Argentina and India.

Into combat!

It was not long before events in the Middle East saw two of the former Cottesmore squadrons 15 and 44, employed operationally for the first time. On 26 June 1956 President Nasser of Egypt announced the nationalisation of the Suez Canal Company to the dismay of the British, French and Israeli Governments who still felt that they had vital interests in the region. On 29 October, Israel attacked Egypt across the Sinai Peninsular. The next day the British and French Governments issued an ultimatum to Israel and Egypt to stop hostilities within 24 hours and withdraw troops 10 miles from the Suez Canal to allow occupation of Port Said, Ismailia and Suez by Franco-British Forces. 15 and 44 squadrons flew to Cyprus to join 10, 18, 27 and 61 squadrons.

The situation in Cyprus was complicated by the ancient feud between Greeks and Turks. The Greek community led by Archbishop Makarios was trying to achieve union with Greece (Enosis). This

Squadron Leader I. G. Broom, Officer Commanding 57 Squadron. *(Photo: MoD)*

Resting between sorties is a 44 Squadron Canberra B2 WH920 sometime during 1955 - note the Cottesmore Wing markings on the fin. *(Photo: E Watts)*

was opposed by the Turks with the utmost ferocity. A Greek underground organisation known as Eoka, led by Colonel Grivas, was trying to influence matters by eliminating as many British servicemen (who happened to be in the middle) as possible. The bomber aircrews who had left the UK too abruptly to be issued with such niceties as KD, were issued, soon after arrival, with a revolver and several rounds of ammunition which they sported about their person in various incongruous combinations of RAF winter wear in the late summer heat to the immense amusement and pleasure of the bronzed night fighter and 39 Squadron crews dazzling in their smart KD uniforms.

On the evening of 31 October the bomber crews were briefed on their targets - all airfields: Cairo West, Almaza, Bilbeis and Inchas; the Cyprus aircraft going in at medium level. They were told that the Egyptian Air Force had 80 Russian built Mig-15 fighters and 45 IL-28 bombers, 25 British built Meteor and Vampire fighters and about 200 transport and training aircraft with radar predicted guns protecting the airfields. After the briefing the crews went back to their messes for a pre-flight meal, to hear on the radio the 'Voice of Cyprus' warning all Egyptians to avoid the vicinity of airfields. This thought provoking message was repeated every few moments. This was a sporting gesture, since the Canberras were at 15,000 feet or thereabouts, a comfortable height for the defending Meteors, Vampires and Migs.

The first aircraft started to roll as dusk was falling, with the setting sun to starboard dipping into the horizontal hazy air. The navigators were relying entirely on dead reckoning navigation supplemented where possible by visual pin points from the bomb aimer in the nose, though as things turned out it was not necessary. They had been preceded by 18 Squadron and 139 Squadron who had dropped markers, and could clearly see the target indicators almost before they had reached the top of the climb. The markers used the system pioneered by Mickey Martin and Leonard Cheshire of 617 Squadron using Lancasters in 1944; the Canberras did the job at least as well, they were lighter and better adapted to it. The master bomber peeled off from about 4,000 feet into a shallow dive with the pilot aiming the whole aircraft at the target and releasing the markers himself from about 400 feet. It was very accurate. Barely two hours after take off, the Cyprus aircraft were back on the ground with much of that time spent on an elaborate let down designed to separate the aircraft into reasonable intervals. The next day the process was repeated on other airfields including Fayid and Abu Sueir and on Cairo Radio.

Air reconnaissance at the end of the second day showed that, except for 10 IL-28 bombers which had been evacuated, the majority of the Egyptian combat aircraft had been put out of action on the ground. Only one RAF aircraft had been attacked in the air suffering slight damage and one or two others were damaged by anti-aircraft fire. One 61 Squadron crew did suddenly find itself in disarray, inverted and heading for the desert. The pilot regained control, presumably after flak had tipped him over. The crew returned to Nicosia shaken if not stirred.

The evacuated IL-28 bombers were found by reconnaissance aircraft on Luxor airfield and were attacked the following day. With one hour of daylight and 2 hours and 40 minutes night flying, there was time to look around, particularly on the way back. What appeared at first to be a dead straight road gleaming in the moonlight was in fact the Suez Canal - the cause of all the fuss. Shortly afterwards British and French paratroops took Port Said.

On 6 November, primarily as a result of American and United Nations pressure, but also as the result of opposition in the UK Parliament, a cease fire took effect and the Franco-British forces handed the Canal over to a United Nations peacekeeping force.

Cottesmore had been earmarked for development as a V-Bomber base. The three short runways were inadequate; instead one long 3,000 yard runway was constructed, new taxiways and dispersals, new Air Traffic Control facilities such as Instrument Landing System (ILS), Cathode Ray Direction Finding (CRDF) and Ground Controlled Approach (GCA) radar, new engineering facilities and by March 1958 Cottesmore was ready to accept its first Handley Page Victor.

CHAPTER FIVE

The V-Force arrives.

A Victor B1A of 15 Squadron drops 35 1000 pound bombs *(Photo: MoD)*

With the Canberra, Cottesmore had emerged from its training role into the front line of RAF operations. In December 1957 it became clear that it was being groomed to assume the mantle of spearhead and showpiece of the RAF. The C-in-C Bomber Command, Sir Harry Broadhurst, announced that subject to Air Ministry approval, the first two Victor squadrons would form at Cottesmore in the second quarter of 1958. They were however not the first type of V-Bomber to operate from the base.

Four Valiant aircraft from 90 Squadron and two from 199 Squadron were attached to Cottesmore while the runway at Honington was being serviced from the 5th until 26 March 1958. This was a useful exercise for all parties, permitting experience to be gained with the new airfield aids: CRDF, ILS, CPN18 and ACR7 and with the new VHF Jet Letdown procedures controlled by RAF Wittering. The extensive reconstruction of the airfield, the new 9,003 feet long main runway, new taxiways, dispersals and fuel installations involved the absorbtion of a local road from Cottesmore to Market Overton. Cottesmore received its first Victor on 9 April 1958 and Group Captain J E 'Johnnie' Johnson (DSO and 2 bars, DFC and bar, American DFC, Legion of Merit, Air Medal, Belgian Legion of Honour and Croix de Guerre, top scoring British fighter pilot with 38 confirmed victories during WWII) took command from Wing Commander M H Le Bas DSO AFC.

The first aircraft, Victor B1 XA935, was collected from the manufacturer's airfield at Radlett by the CO of 10 Squadron, Wing Commander C B Owen DSO DFC AFC and his crew, Flying Officer Galbraith (2nd pilot), Flight Lieutenants Wardley and Hoxey (navigators) and Flight Lieutenant Bannister (AEO). The Squadron was reformed on 15 April. The second aircraft, XA927, arrived a week later and a further two (XA928 and XA936) arrived during May. Newly trained crews arrived from Gaydon throughout May, June and July, and the eighth and last aircraft was collected on 9 September.

The aircraft were popular with the aircrew who particularly liked the crew compartment. As with the other V-Bombers, the Valiant and the Avro Vulcan, the navigators and Air Electronics Operators (AEOs) faced rearwards and did not have ejection seats, but unlike the other two the crew were together in one compartment, on the same level. As Wing Commander Owen remarked:

'Being able to glance over ones shoulder and see everyone else gives a feeling of compactness and a sense of crew unity that you don't get when the crews are separated and their only link is the intercom.'

At this point it may be asked why was it necessary to indulge in the enormous expense of developing such a powerful force when we should have been moving forward into a 'broadly based period of peace'. Russia's acquisition of atomic weapons and the Communist advances in the Far East more than anything prompted the British Government to adopt Theodore Roosevelt's adage: 'Speak softly and carry a big stick'. The stick was the independent nuclear deterrent and the method of transportation was the V-Bomber.

The first British atomic warhead was successfully tested in the Monte Bello Islands on 2 October 1952 but the V-bombers had been in development for some time. In 1946 the Air Ministry produced a specification for a long range bomber with a 1,500 nm radius of action, a cruise speed of 500 knots and a height above the target of 45,000 feet. With the possibility of impending disaster in Korea, a less demanding specification was drawn up to produce an aircraft more quickly - the result was the Valiant.

The first Valiant touched down at Gaydon on 8 February 1955 just four years and five months after Vickers had received its first production order. Four types of V-aircraft actually flew; the Short Sperrin (of which only two prototypes were built), the Valiant, the Vulcan and the Victor. 15 April 1958, the official date of the inauguration of the Victor at Cottesmore was significant for the RAF. From that time all three production V- Bombers were in service with Bomber Command: three remarkable aircraft. The delta wing Vulcan was perhaps the most dramatic in appearance, but the graceful crescent-winged Victor with the high swept tailplane powered by four Armstrong Siddeley Sapphire 7 Mk 202 engines was also striking in appearance and according to several publications, including the programme for the Cottesmore Open Day of that year, the first supersonic bomber, although not flown above the speed of sound in squadron service. The Valiant, the stop gap aircraft was more mundane, if business-like in appearance. By the end of 1958 there were 156 aircraft in 15 squadrons in the V-Force.

The third Victor for 10 Squadron, a B1 - serialled XA928 takes off from Cottesmore on 10 September 1958. *(Photo MoD)*

A beautiful view of XH588, a 15 Squadron Victor B1 taken during July 1959, showing the crescent wing form to perfection. *(Photo:MoD)*

The main force Valiants were at Wittering (Nos 9 and 138 squadrons), Marham (49, 148, 207 and 214 squadrons) and Honington (90 Squadron). Vulcans were at Scampton (27, 83 and 617 squadrons) and Waddington (44, 50 and 101 squadrons) and the Victors were at Honington (55 and 57 squadrons) and at Cottesmore (10 and 15 squadrons), the latter squadron having arrived in September. In addition Gaydon, Finningley and Wyton had V-Force aircraft in other than main force roles.

With such a complex leap forward in technology there were some initial teething problems. On 30 July 1958 the Victors were grounded for the tailplanes to be removed and returned to the manufacturers for modification after cracks had been found during routine servicing. Another significant defect was found at Cottesmore which affected all Victor aircraft. This was a seizure of the input limiting guide to the powered flying control. Both the faults were corrected and by 19 August crews were able to restart training. Flight Lieutenant Richardson and crew, who had been nominated as the display crew for the SBAC Show at Farnborough in September, were now able to start training for the first of a whole series of publicity events for the aircraft and the new 'big jet' RAF. The 10 Squadron aircrew flew in a 'Vic' formation with examples of the other two V-Bombers on every day of the SBAC show, except on the 3rd and 4th which were cancelled due to weather. Other high profile events that month included an ITV programme, filmed at Cottesmore entitled 'The Heavyweights' and a large scale press visit to the station. By far the biggest and most complex operation took place on 19 September when the Station opened its gates for a 'Battle of Britain at Home Day'. Aided by all the publicity which preceded it, this event proved to be highly popular with the public.

On a sharp, sunny but windy day, over 40,000 people headed for Cottesmore jamming the approach roads in all directions. Over 13,000 cars drove onto the airfield and over 1,000 people travelled by train. They enjoyed a 40 item flying display which provided both spectacle and a touch of drama (for two people at least) when a Jet Provost flamed out at the top of a loop. The pilot executed a copy book dead stick landing and many of the crowd were unaware that anything untoward had taken place. There was a large static display, numerous sideshows, a BEA helicopter giving joy rides, a link trainer for would-be pilots to try their hand and passenger carrying model trains. At the end of the day, the RAF Benevolent Fund was better off by a respectable sum to help further its excellent work.

10 Squadron provided aircraft for 'Battle of Britain At Home' events and elsewhere, including Heathrow Airport. Perhaps it was not surprising that at the end of this hectic month the 540 compiling officer should note ruefully: *The primary role of the squadron was rather neglected during this month due to excessive Station commitments involving displays and formation flying'.*

15 Squadron also reformed with Victor B1s at Cottesmore, on 1 September 1958. The first aircraft, XA941, was collected by the CO, Wing Commander D A Green DSO OBE DFC and his crew from Radlett on 16 September. They returned to Gaydon immediately afterwards to complete their conversion course, and the aircraft was swooped on by the Cottesmore engineers for acceptance checks.

15 Squadron has a distinguished history. It had been in France with BE2s in June 1916 for only eight days when it lost its first pilot, Captain V H N Wadham who was shot dead during an aerial combat. His observer, Sergeant Piper who had observed the occurrence with some concern from the rear cockpit, climbed out of his seat and into the pilot's cockpit. Sitting on the dead pilot's lap, he managed to regain control and put the aircraft down behind the German lines. Losing a little of his sang froid at the last moment he jumped clear of the aircraft just before it hit the ground and was taken prisoner.

When, in April 1941, the Squadron converted from Wellingtons to Stirlings, one of the new aircraft was 'MacRobert's Reply', the aircraft given by Lady MacRobert in memory of her three sons all of whom were killed flying with the RAF. The aircraft flew on the Squadron's first mission in the new type to Berlin on the night of 30 April/1 May 1941. En route for another operation at this time the crews dropped packets of tea from Batavia in the Dutch East Indies for the people of Holland with messages of good will and encouragement. At the end of the war the Squadron's last tasks were to fly enough food to Holland to feed 26,000 people together with further packets of tea. All this was done in one week, in operations that gave the crews enormous satisfaction. The tradition of 'MacRobert's Reply' continues to the present day on one of the Squadron's Tornado aircraft at RAF Laarbruch.

VIP Visitors

Before the newly trained Victor crews were able to give their undivided attention to their primary task there were other ceremonial commitments to be completed when Princess Margaret presented a new standard to 10 Squadron on 21 October 1958. On 1 April 1959 the Prime Minister, Mr Harold MacMillan, accompanied by the C-in-C Sir Harry Broadhurst, AOC 3 Group Air Vice-Marshal K B B Cross and the Station Commander, reviewed the Station. Amongst other things, he met the Victor crews and then scrambled four of the aircraft. This was no mere showpiece. With the latest weaponry it had become clear that any warning of attack would be limited; to counter this the V-Bombers were required to be airborne within a few minutes of receiving a warning.

To achieve a rapid start the engines were later modified to start simultaneously. With practice it became normal for four aircraft to be airborne within four minutes of a signal from Bomber Command. On this occasion they were all airborne in 3 minutes 50 seconds. Operational Readiness Platforms (ORPs) were build at all V-Bomber stations and all dispersal airfields from which aircraft could roll a few feet on to the runway. The scramble of the V-Bombers then, while having a deadly operational point, also became one of the attractions of the annual 'At Home Days' and a spectacle for distinguished visitors. Others who followed that spring, were King Hussein of Jordon on 24 April and the Shah of Persia on 13 May. King Hussein, an experienced pilot, flew in Victor XA938 with OC 10 Squadron from Cottesmore to Farnborough at the end of his visit. But it was not all ceremony. The crews began their classification in aircraft handling, bombing and navigation. The pattern of training at Cottesmore

Above Left: King Hussein of Jordan, accompanied by the Station Commander Group Captain 'Johnnie' Johnson inspects the Guard of Honour during the Kings's visit to the station on 24 April 1959. *Above Right:* The King says farewell to ACM Sir Harry Broadhurst just before departing the Station in Victor XA938 with the Officer Commanding 10 Squadron, Wing Commander Owen.

Below: The Princess Margaret, escorted by the C-in-C Bomber Command ACM Sir Harry Broadhurst and the Station Commander 'Johnnie' Johnson after her arrival for the presentation of the 10 Squadron Standard on 21 October 1958. *(Photo's: MoD)*

A further important visior was The Shah of Persia, seen here accompanied by the Station Commander, Group Captain 'Johnnie' Johnson, meeting the crew of a Canberra during a visit to the station on 13 May 1959. *(Photo: MoD)*

and in the V-Force as a whole, comprised cross country flights which included radar bombing and a whole series of Station, Group and Command exercises designed to practise arming and dispersing followed by flight profiles of likely operational missions simulating failures in various items of equipment. Some of the names will be familiar to many now leading less energetic lives: Bombex, Compex, Kingpin, Kinsman, Mayflight, Mick, Mickey Finn, Sunspot, Yeoman etc.

Training Exercises.
Group Exercises began in earnest at Cottesmore on 4 November 1958. Four aircraft (three from 10 Squadron, one from 15 Squadron) took off for the exercise which comprised Navigation Bombing System/Radar Bombing System (NBS/RBS) attacks on three targets and two navigation stages. The first Exercise Mick involving the practice of all the alert and readiness measures, the arming of aircraft and the scramble to fly on operational profiles took place between 2nd and 6th March 1959.

The first Victor Lone Ranger took off for Akrotiri, Cyprus, on 21 April 1959 with Group Captain Johnson and Wing Commander Green at the controls. They flew the 2,210 miles in under four hours, (30 minutes quicker than the standing unofficial record time). They returned on 23 April, landing at Waddington (presumably for customs clearance) against the wind, 4 hours 45 minutes after take off. Others quickly followed, to Akrotiri, Wildenrath in Germany and the first Western Ranger to Goose Bay, Labrador, and Offutt Air Base in Nebraska, the headquarters of Strategic Air Command.

The Victors first flew in Exercise Mandate, the annual United Kingdom Air Defence Exercise from between 23 and 27 July 1959, participating in major raids against the United Kingdom. There were take-offs all round the clock but the majority were at night when gentlefolk in England were abed and blissfully unaware of the activity that was going on over 40,000 feet above their heads. Nearly all profiles ended with the pilots getting in some Continuation Training: RADAR circuits, PAR approaches, ILS approaches, internal aids approaches, visual circuits, practice engine failures, powered flying controls failures, so that by the time the aircraft had landed every member of the crew had thoroughly exercised his trade.

Many V-Force crews came to know Goose Bay in Labrador well, in all its changing seasons. After the confines of an aircrew's crew compartment, the air was clean and rare. In the summertime the floatplanes would skim across the bay leaving plumes of silver spray and everywhere the smell of birch and pines. In the winter it was gripped in a cold so sharp that the hairs in ones nose went stiff and white, the bay, the lakes and the sea froze, the roads or tracks ended a little way into the forest and the only way in or out was by air.

In those days Goose Bay was nominally a Canadian Base, but the Americans had the greater share of facilities: more buildings, more transport, more aircraft with a resident force of KC-135 Tankers and Delta Dagger fighters. The Canadians had Voodoo fighters and several propellor driven types including Packets and Lancasters, there were also civilian aircraft passing through and resident Okanagan Airways with helicopters buzzing in and out, prospecting up country for minerals. There were nearly always V-Bombers there, passing outbound to Offutt or inbound to the UK.

On the leg from Goose Bay down to Omaha names like Lake Eon, Bagotville, Sept Iles, Trois Rivieres, Sault St Marie, Iron Mountain, La Crosse, Des Moines and several RBS sites became familiar as simulated RBS attacks were carried out. At Offutt it was usual for the crews to have a day off. W C Fields once said of the City of Brotherly Love: 'I went to Philadelphia but it was closed'. Omaha, which was adjacent to Offutt was a similar sort of place and seasoned crews tended to spend their free day making use of the wide facilities on the base.

The leg over the Atlantic was always interesting for navigators; they had to work harder for peace of mind over a large stretch of water, and Goose Bay was quite near to the North Magnetic Pole which sometimes made the magnetic compass wobble like a Warrant Officer homing onto a beer call. Over land there was almost an embarrassment of riches in nav aids; over the sea it came to Sun position lines or Sun Moon fixes, monitoring the doppler Green Satin equipment. Wise navigators tended to drift a little north of track to get a long range fix from the NBS on the southern tip of Greenland or a running long range radio compass fix from Prins Christian Sund before looking forward to the landfall ahead.

Nuclear QRA

Quick Reaction Alert (QRA) was introduced at Cottesmore, as it was with the rest of the V-Force, at the beginning of 1962 and lasted until June 1968 when the commitment was taken over by the Royal Navy's Polaris submarines. Each V-Bomber squadron had one aircraft at 15 minutes readiness for 24 hours every day of the year. Crew caravans were located alongside the dispersals where QRA crews spent much of their time; from here they were exercised by the Bomber Controller at least once during their tour of duty.

An example of one of the Bomber Command exercises which preceded the QRA introduction was Exercise Mayflight which took place between 4 May and 8 May 1959, involving the dispersal of four 10 Squadron aircraft to Boscombe Down and four 15 Squadron aircraft to St Mawgan. Transport Command aircraft flew out the maintenance teams who prepared the Victors for immediate action. On a signal from Bomber Command the eight dispersed aircraft and as many more as possible at Cottesmore scrambled for normal profile flights with NBS attacks against selected targets, navigation stages and the usual continuation training on return to base. There were three practice alerts; one to engine start, two to start and taxi to take-off point (one day, one night) and finally the scramble itself. The crews never knew how far along the path they would go before they were stood down (temporarily); sometimes it was to cockpit readiness, to engine start, to taxi, to roll or to take-off.

The deadly serious business was interspersed by overseas flights throughout 1959. In May a crew flew to Westover Air Force Base, Massachusetts, for a static display at the 'Armed Forces Day', in

June a crew flew to Lisbon for a display at the British Trade Fair, in July two 15 Squadron Victors supported by a Comet of 216 Squadron flew to Vancouver to give displays at Royal Canadian Air Force and Canadian Department of Transport Ceremonies to commemorate the 50th anniversary of powered flight in Canada. This operation was led by Air Vice-Marshal M H Dwyer CBE, AOC of No 3 Group, flying the lead aircraft with Wing Commander Green in the left hand seat.

The practice of taking one and sometimes two crew chiefs and a bomb bay pannier containing the most obvious spares on overseas flights gave the crews an unsupported flexibility of a high order in the most remote of locations, and many crews learned how to change wheels and carry out quite intricate engineering tasks under the skilled guidance of the crew chief. In addition, an excellent supply organisation developed for express delivery of the more unusual items of spares to V-aircraft on the ground (VOG), so that it was extremely rare for a V-aircraft to return to base more than 24 hours late.

The 1959 Cottesmore 'At Home Day' on 19 September attracted more visitors than in 1958 with an estimated 46,000 passing through the gates all round the perimeter on to the airfield. The morning was wrapped in a drizzly mist but brightened after noon so that the lively air show was enjoyed not only by the throng on the airfield but by an ITV television audience.

Another annual event was the Bomber Command Bombing Competition which took place in 1959 on 28, 29 and 30 September. This was always a severe test of navigation and bombing skills and of teamwork. Two crews from each squadron flew on each of the designated nights on profile missions which included a primary navigation stage, three NBS/RBS bombing attacks and an astro navigation stage. 10 Squadron ended the competition in 6th place overall and 15 Squadron in 11th place with Flight Lieutenant Richardson's crew individually in 3rd place for navigation out of 69 crews. The competition developed to include, from May 1960, competitors from America when the 6th Bombardment Wing participated with their B-52s. The best RAF crews were later invited to take part in the Strategic Air Command Combat Bombing Competition. It became a matter of razor sharp competition and some prestige to be selected after a rigorous eliminating qualifying system; to win one of the trophies was a source of immense satisfaction.

Overseas detachments

On 18 December 1959, Group Captain Johnson handed over command to Group Captain A D Mitchell DFC AFC who had come from the Queen's Flight. 10 Squadron also had a new CO by this time; Wing Commander R B Phillips DFC AFC who flew to Gan and back on 1st to 7 June 1960 to check its suitability as a base for Victor operations. Gan was a tiny coral island only one and three quarters miles long and three quarters of a mile wide. It was the most southerly of the islands in the Addu Atoll in the Maldive Islands about half way between Aden and Singapore. The CO found that it was satisfactory, even though the runway started at one end of the island and ended at the other; abruptly. So did the crews who came to use it extensively as a regular staging post for V-Bomber crews heading for Butterworth in Malaya, Singapore, Australia, New Zealand and points east. Gan had a fringe of drunkenly reeling palm trees on one side of the island from which huge fruit bats hung upside down in strange festoons among the branches gliding silently down with the setting of the sun in search of food. About 600 RAF men were based there in its heyday, and one, rarely seen, woman welfare officer. Presumably she spent much of her time in hiding.

Having found the island suitable for their purpose as a staging post, the first Exercise Profiteer was mounted by 10 Squadron on 19 July 1960. The object of the exercise was to give the medium bomber crews operating experience in the Far East and to provide for a rapid reinforcement of the Far East Air Force (FEAF) should it become necessary. The four Victors originally planned to fly to Butterworth in Malaya via Nairobi municipal airport in Kenya but following disturbances in the Congo and elsewhere in Africa, Nairobi was too overcrowded with civilian air traffic and the route finally

A fine study of three Victor B1's of 15 Squadron in 1959 (Photo: MoD)

flown was Akrotiri in Cyprus, across Turkey to Mauripur (Karachi) Pakistan to Gan and thence to Butterworth. Butterworth, with it's new 8,000 foot north/south runway, was at that time a base for Sabre units of the Royal Australian Air Force. After gaining some very useful experience in operating in humid, tropical conditions, the Victors returned to Cottesmore on 12 August.

It was 15 Squadron's turn to head east in September when four Victors left for Akrotiri on the first of a series of Exercise Sunspots on the 12th of the month. These exercises were intended to give the medium and light bomber crews (V-Force and Canberra) experience in operating from Mediterranean bases. The aircraft returned on 17 October 1960. These exercises were preludes to later active service operations by Cottesmore aircraft in the Middle and Far East.

While 10 Squadron were away on their Sunspot Exercise in January and February 1961 an important trial on centralised and progressive servicing was begun at Cottesmore, which revolutionised the servicing methods on V-Force Stations. Until this time each squadron had its own groundcrews. A crew chief was assigned to each aircraft, many had followed its construction through the factory 'from a heap of nuts and bolts', and remained with it for many years as the trusted mentor for the aircrew. Names of aircrew and crew chief were painted on the aircraft and while the aircrew found themselves from time to time flying in other aircraft, the crew chief stayed with his aircraft and followed it to second and third line servicing.

The trial tested the possibilities of operating with all the station aircraft in a centralised system with the use of a master controller to coordinate all aircraft requirements. It allowed for the re-deployment of technical manpower and the operation of an 18 hour day by the second line organisation and produced a much smoother flow of work. The Cottesmore progressive servicing schedule also produced advantages, allowing servicing to be carried out in far better conditions in well lit and dry hangars by day and by night. As the report calmly commented: *'servicing an aircraft on wet, windy and cold dispersals in many cases with the aid of torches is not condusive to efficient servicing or flight safety'.*

The new Victor.

It was a complicated technical change vitally dependent on a good communications system but the six months trial proved that it had significant advantages. In addition to its ability to achieve a more rapid turn round of aircraft, it gave a much greater flexibility in their utilisation. On the other hand the Squadron Commanders sometimes felt a sense of frustration in being so dependent on a central organisation for the production of aircraft. It had been thought that the groundcrew might suffer some deterioration in morale, losing their squadron identity, but they found that this obvious disadvantage was more than adequately balanced by the greatly improved working conditions. The scheme was subsequently adopted by the V-Force as a whole.

No 15 Squadron received a new version of the aircraft, the B1A, during July 1960. This aircraft, XH613, differed primarily from the earlier model by being equipped with more sophisticated radar and electronic counter measures (ECM) equipment. Eventually, the Squadron became entirely equipped with this version of the Victor, some of which were modified B1s, receiving its eighth and last aircraft, XH587, on 15 January 1962.

When an improved version of the Victor, the B2, was about to enter squadron service in 1961, Cottesmore was chosen as the training base for the crews. This aircraft was a significant advance on the B1, having wings of greater span, and much more powerful Rolls-Royce Conway bypass turbofan engines of 19,750 pounds of thrust compared with the 11,000 pounds of the Armstrong Siddeley Sapphires. Initially, 'C' Flight, 232 Operational Conversion Unit (OCU), was formed to convert former B1 crews onto the aircraft for new squadrons. 'C' Flight, known as 'C' Squadron, formed following the delivery of XL188, the first B2 to enter service with Bomber Command, on 1 November 1961, the units fourth and last aircraft, XL230, arriving on 19 December. The first two graduate crews left Cottesmore

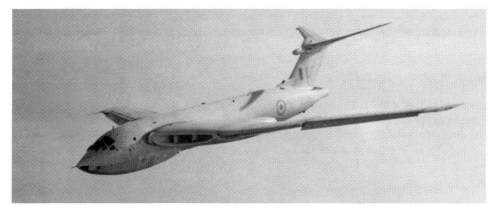

XL165, a Victor B2 of 'C' Flight 232 OCU. *(Photo:MoD)*

on 26 January 1962 for Wittering, Cambridgeshire, to form initially 139 Squadron, the first Victor B2 squadron, which reformed on 1 February. Conversion training continued, but on 17 April, 'C' Squadron commenced an Intensive Flying Trial (IFT) with its four B2s, when 1,000hrs flying had to be completed within 60 days. Sorties, as long as seven hours, seven days a week until midnight, were flown, utilising recently trained crews from Wittering, and student crews. Exceptional reliability enabled the IFT to be completed in 48 days, the final hours being flown when all four aircraft were airborne at the same time, on 3 June. On completion of the IFT, 'C' Squadron's role was solely crew conversion.

A new Station Commander arrived in February 1962 when Group Captain A D Mitchell CVO DFC AFC handed over to Group Captain R H G Weighill DFC who had already made something of a name for himself on the rugby field. He captained the England Rugby XV in 1948 and later played for the British Lions.

The Station suffered two set backs in June 1962 when each of the operational squadrons lost an aircraft in widely differing circumstances. On 14 June XH613, flown by Wing Commander Matthews, CO of 15 Squadron crashed at Swayfield, five miles short of the runway returning from a Groupex. The crew survived with relatively minor injuries and were taken to the RAF Hospital at Nocton Hall near Lincoln. Wing Commander Matthews was able to return to duty. After a period of treatment the injured crew were sent to the RAF Medical Rehabilitation Unit at Headley Court in Surrey where they were eased back into the system. The crew of the other aircraft were not so fortunate. Just two days later, XA929 captained by Flight Lieutenant G A Goatham of 10 Squadron crashed on take-off from Akrotiri. This time there was no time to abandon the aircraft and all six members of the crew were killed.

The Cuban crisis

By 1962 the V-Force had become a tremendously experienced, efficient and formidable force in a number of roles world wide, although its primary role remained nuclear deterrence. When the harsh sounds of a general alert rent the air on 27 October 1962, the station moved smoothly to a state of readiness following the usual well drilled procedures of Group and Command exercises. The alert stages progressed, the number of QRA aircraft were increased until slowly the chilling realisation penetrated that it was no exercise. It was real.

Russia had supplied missiles to Cuba. President Kennedy reacted with resolution to this threat to the American mainland. He decided on a naval blockage of Cuba. As the two fleets approached each other, the whole deterrent force was brought to readiness. Suddenly the Russian leader, Nikita Krushchev, backed away and ordered his ships back to Russia. At Cottesmore and at all the other V-Bomber bases the tension relaxed and everything returned to normal save for the QRA crews who

Krushchev, backed away and ordered his ships back to Russia. At Cottesmore and at all the other V-Bomber bases the tension relaxed and everything returned to normal save for the QRA crews who continued their vigil.

Cottesmore is the second highest RAF airfield in the UK (after RAF Lyneham), at 461 feet above sea level and, from time to time, suffers from severe winter weather. The east wind from December to April is keener than the west and infinitely more unpleasant. Group Captain Weighill was moved to write the following in the February 1963 Form 540:

'I should like to record that from 21 December 1962 until 25 February 1963, this station experienced the worst weather known in this part of the country during the whole of the century. For days at a time there were blizzard conditions, and for weeks the temperature did not rise above freezing point. In addition the almost unknown hazard of freezing rain occurred on several occasions, enveloping roads, taxiways, runways, vehicles and aircraft in a film of hard, clear ice. The difficulties of operating in these most trying conditions were tremendous and were only overcome by long hours of hard work in the most trying conditions by all ranks of the station. It is worthy of note that during the whole time there were only short periods when the freezing rain was at its worst that the airfield became non operational, and even then I consider that I could have launched the QRA aircraft had there been sufficient urgency.'

Borneo, Malaya and Cyprus.

The 1960 Exercise Profiteers were succeeded by Exercise Chamfrom detachments when 10 Squadron aircraft flew out to Butterworth on 21 January 1963 to reinforce the FEAF at the time of the Borneo Campaign and the Indonesian Confrontation with the newly independent state of Malaysia.

In order to make a viable economic unit in its independence from Britain, it was sought to unite Malaya, Sarawak, Borneo and Singapore into the state of Malaysia. A revolt in the small British Protectorate of Brunei in North Borneo and incursions by Indonesian guerrillas aided by Chinese communists into Sarawak and Sabah started the emergency which the British forces quickly moved in to control. Much of the close support work was carried out by 20 Squadron Hunters on detachment to Labuan, 45 Squadron Canberras, 66 Squadron Belvederes and Twin Pioneers flown out from Aden, but the Victors capable of carrying 35 1,000 pound bombs served as a powerful deterrent to any large scale nonesense - they were careful to demonstrate this capability in a well publicised demonstration for the Malayan head of state.

The rotating Cottesmore squadrons usually flew out via Akrotiri (Cyprus), Khormaksar (Aden) and Gan to either Singapore (Tengah) or Butterworth. They prepared for action by training at low and high level, sometimes flying low to pop up and drop 1,000 pounders on Song Song and China Rock ranges off the east coast of Malaya. Crews were rotated more frequently than the aircraft, the usual length of detachment being two to three months with the duty coming up about twice a year.

These flights not only had serious political and military objectives as well as providing valuable training opportunities, but also offered a bonus of exotic travel experiences for the squadron. Aden was always a jolt to the senses with its grinding poverty.

Butterworth and Tengah were just about the greenest places most people had ever seen. The tropical heat was however a welcome relief to the arctic conditions at home, and it was no doubt with some pleasure that Group Captain Weighill flew out to Butterworth to visit the 10 Squadron detachment on 14 February 1963.

The period between 1960 and 1964 was marked by an acceleration in the 'winds of change' that were blowing through Africa. Ten countries with over 75 million inhabitants achieved independence from Britain at this time. Kenya and Zanzibar were two of them. Two 10 Squadron Victors captained by Wing Commander T C Gledhill AFC and Flight Lieutenant K W Rooney arrived at Nairobi on 4

Malakal, Khartoum and 'Nasser's Corner' to El Adem for refuelling.

Two days after their departure, two pairs of 15 Squadron Victors were called prematurely to Tengah for a Chamfrom detachment as conditions there deteriorated: Wing Commander W G S Marshall and Flying Officer J R Bowman and crews left on the 5th and Squadron Leader D Mullarkey MBE and Flight Lieutenant T G Murphy and crews followed on the 6th. 15 Squadron maintained a detachment of four Victors, five crews and ground support personnel in Malaya continuously until October 1964 and activity also remained high at Cottesmore until 2359 hrs on 1 March 1964 when 10 Squadron was officially disbanded. 'C' Flight 232 OCU had moved over the Rutland border to Wittering on 31 March 1963 to join the Victor B2 Wing there. The last 15 Squadron Chamfrom detachment returned from Butterworth in October. The crews had been kept busy until the end following the state of emergency which was declared in Malaysia after Indonesian landings at Pontian and Labis. The crews had been brought to a high state of readiness and the aircraft had been dispersed to reduce the effects of possible air attack. On 15 September two of the aircraft, with a support party, were dispersed to Gan where they remained in readiness until recalled on 27 September. The last crews returned to Cottesmore on 3 October. 15 Squadron had been declared non-operational from 1 October, and was disbanded on 31 October 1964. A Guest Night, to mark this occasion and the departure of Group Captain Weighill to HQ RAF Germany, was held at which the Senior Air Staff Officer (SASO), 3 Group, Air Commodore Burton CBE DSO represented the AOC. Most of the aircraft were returned to Radlett from whence they had come, save for XH615 which went to Honington and XA940 to Gaydon.

This was the end of the Victor at Cottesmore but it was by no means the end of the useful life of these majestic aircraft. They were converted into Flight Refuelling Tankers, and took over the role from the Valiants at Marham. Only now in the 1990s is its life coming to an end as VC10s and Tristars take over the tanking commitment.

The Vulcan.

The Vulcan must be the most unmistakeable aircraft: in shape, size, power, in its ungainly stance on the ground with three enormous stilted legs, and in the air a delta shape like something from a novel by H G Wells; even the most disinterested of wives would recognise it instantly. Or would have done in the late 1950's, 60's, 70's and early 80's. In November 1964 the Vulcan arrived at Cottesmore to dominate the Rutland skies when three B2 squadrons, 9, 12 and 35, flew in from Coningsby to replace 10 and 15 Victor squadrons. They then formed the Cottesmore Wing, and brought with them the centralised servicing system that had been introduced while they had been at Coningsby, with the units not having individual aircraft allocated to them.

35 Squadron had earlier been one of the first two squadrons that had flown into Cottesmore on 20 April 1938, almost six weeks after the Station had opened. On 28 November 1966 it celebrated its 50th Anniversary, and was older than the RAF itself, having been part of the Royal Flying Corps eighteen months before the RAF had formed on 1 April 1918.

The Vulcan, produced by A V Roe and designed by a team led by Sir William Farren was powered by the magnificent Bristol Olympus engine. This, the first real twin-spool axial turbojet was almost as great a leap forward over the Canberra's Avon as that engine had been over the Meteor's Derwent. The Design team developed the Mark 101 Olympus, rated at 11,000 pounds of thrust which powered the prototype Vulcan, up to the 20,000 pounds plus thrust of the 300 Series engines, which powered the Vulcan B2s of the three Cottesmore squadrons, making them the most powerful (and most reliable) engines in the RAF.

The Vulcan was a fine aircraft: a multi-role combat aircraft before the design of a multi-role combat aircraft. In its time a high and low level bomber in the nuclear and conventional roles, a strategic reconnaissance aircraft, a stand off missile carrier, a maritime reconnaissance aircraft, a tanker and

77

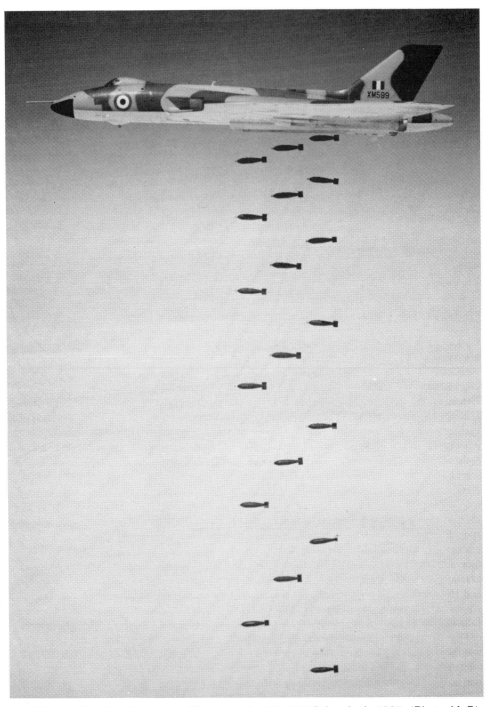

A Vulcan B2 of the Cottesmore Wing sropping 21 1000 lb bombs in 1965. *(Photo: MoD)*

even on occasion an interceptor. Right at the end of its career, in May 1982, literally a few weeks before they were due to be scrapped, the Vulcan was called upon to carry out the longest operational bombing sorties by any aircraft in any air force when it flew several 7,860 mile round trips from Ascension Island to attack the Argentine occupation forces at Port Stanley in the Falkland Islands and denied the use of its runway to the Argentine Mirages, Skyhawks and Super Etendards with their Exocet Missiles.

The aircraft that flew into Cottesmore on that November day in 1964 were painted in the grey and green camouflage upper surfaces to go with their recently introduced low level role. This training, for which the aircraft had never been designed, started nine months before at Coningsby led by the CO of 35 Squadron, Wing Commander D B Craig (now Chief of Defence Staff MRAF Sir David Craig GCB, OBE, MA, FRAeS).

They arrived at a time of local changes in Rutland: there was a move to merge Rutland into the surrounding counties of Lincolnshire, Cambridgeshire, Northants etc in the bureaucratic cause of efficiency. This brought out their fighting qualities and they resisted with the utmost ferocity. Led by Sir George Ruddle, the brewer of Langham, they succeeded for a time and celebrated their victory by drinking a special 'Victory Ale' produced by the Ruddles brewery. But it was only a temporary respite and in 1974 Rutland was absorbed into Leicestershire.

The three squadrons quickly settled into their routines at Cottesmore and on 17 November 1964 the new Station Commander, Group Captain E W Wright CBE DFC DFM, reported that the Vulcan Wing was fully operational with Quick Reaction Alert (QRA) mounted. 12 Squadron had already taken over the Chamfrom Detachment from the Victors of 15 Squadron, where four of their aircraft had been operating from Butterworth since September 1964.

Routine training continued until 1600 hours on 26 April 1965 when without warning Cottesmore was ordered to prepare eight aircraft for a rapid reinforcement to the Far East. The first aircraft took off at 0045 hours the next morning and by 0623 hours all eight aircraft were airborne and a further four aircraft were prepared. They arrived at Gan between 0230 hours and 1038 hours on the 28th. From here HQ FEAF split the force up, sending four to Tengah and four to Butterworth. The Captains of the crews were the CO of 35 Squadron, Wing Commander D B Craig, Wing Commander Pollington, Flight Lieutenant Ness, Flight Lieutnant Downs, Flight Lieutenant Gallwey, Flight Lieutenant Lloyd, Flight Lieutenant Frankin and Flight Lieutenant J P L'Estrange (he must have enjoyed flying the Vulcan because he was still flying the aircraft at Waddington as a Squadron Leader in the early 1980s until they were retired from the service). Before the crews had left Cottesmore, they were briefed on the situation by the AOC 1 Group, Air Vice-Marshal D C Stapleton CB CBE, DFC, AFC.

The birth pangs of Malaysia had been worse than most and it was at this time that Singapore decided to secede from the federation. This seemed to act as a spur to Indonesian ambitions. Their sporadic guerilla activity and incursions into Malaysian airspace were increased and reinforced by seaborne raids on mainland Malaysia and by the dropping of paratroops near Labis. As tension mounted the Chamfrom detachment became the Matterhorn Rotation which called for up to 24 Vulcans to reinforce the FEAF: 8 aircraft and 10 aircrews, servicing support and Wing Ops staff to Butterworth and 16 aircraft and 20 aircrews and staff to Tengah. The first two aircraft departed Cottesmore on 6 August for Tengah by way of Akrotiri, Muharraq (Bahrain in the Persian Gulf) and Gan, two more following on the 9th. The technical party left in two Britannias on the 8th and 13th under the command of Flight Lieutenant Harland. An unusual incident marred the successful move of the technicians. This was the untimely death of Corporal A F Frost, an armament fitter who died at RAF Muharraq, Bahrain, while en route. He was buried with full military honours at Muharraq on the 9th before the party hurriedly continued on their way to Gan.

For most of the young men on the aircraft it would have been their first sight of a coral island and the nearest to the Equator they had ever been. With an overnight stay they would have had the

On 26 August 1966, the first Vulcan aircraft and crews returned from the Far East Detachment maintained by the Station during the Confrontation by Indonedisa *(Photo: MoD)*

opportunity of a swim or some scuba diving in the crystal clear water inside the reef. In the early morning before departure they would see the islanders from neighbouring Hitaddu coming to work on Gan in their longboats with gentle curving prows like Viking ships, violently thrashing the water and singing tunelessly in rhythm with the paddle strokes. They would be gone by evening when the islanders ghosted silently the other way with sails unfurled taking advantage of wind and current.

The detachment quickly settled into a steady rhythm of training at Tengah. Later when tension mounted again, a further four Cottesmore aircraft, this time from 12 Squadron slipped unobtrusively out over the Indian Ocean to sit expectantly at Gan waiting to be called. The crisis passed and they returned to England. Each of the three Cottesmore squadrons took their turn at Tengah. When 12 Squadron took over from 35 Squadron on 2 October the detachment had moved up to Butterworth. Orders were received on 14 August 1966 to return to England following the signing of the Bangkok Agreement by Malaysia and Indonesia, ending the confrontation. The captain of the second aircraft to return to Cottesmore on 26 August was Flight Lieutenant B Dorrington; the same Flight Lieutenant Dorrington who retired from Cottesmore in 1988 as an Ops Officer.

Unusual destinations to visit...

There were other duties for the Cottesmore Wing to perform at this time and other unfamiliar places to visit. One was to assist at the opening ceremony of the Auckland International Airport at Mengere, New Zealand. Air Vice-Marshal D C Stapleton CB CBE DFC, AOC 1 Group, flew with Flight Lieutenant Kharegat's crew in XM612 and Flight Lieutenant R D Downs and crew in XM650. They left Cottesmore on 19 January 1966 and flew out via the usual route as far as Tengah and there to Darwin in the Northern Territory of Australia to Fairburn and on to Ohakea the RNZAF base in the North Island of New Zealand. Flight Lieutenant Kharegat carried out a flying display during the ceremony before they

Vulcans from 12/35 Squadron attend the opening of New Zealands new municipal airport at Mangere on 29 January 1966. *(Photo: MoD)*

continued their journey eastwards across the International Date line to Pago Pago in Samoa so that the 3 hour 45 minute flight from Ohakea looked as though it was 27 hours 45 minutes when log books came to be filled in; 24 hours had been lost somewhere. This was not the first time Vulcans had passed this way; the Scampton Wing were the trail blazers in December 1962 when Squadron Leader John Pack and crew of 27 Squadron, Squadron Leader John Sewell of 83 Squadron and Flight Lieutenant Tommy Thompson of 617 Squadron landed on the new runway at Pago Pago after flying past at the opening and closing of the Commonwealth Games in Perth, Western Australia. The next leg to Honolulu was longer: 5 hours 25 minutes which was worth a day off to see Pearl Harbour, Waikiki Beach and try surf riding before continuing to Travis Air Force Base San Francisco. At this time of the year it was sometimes a case of beating the arrival of the fog, especially for the Britannia aircraft following up the Vulcans at a slightly more leisurely pace with the ground crews. After the leg to Offutt the final two flights followed well worn paths to Goose Bay and back across the Atlantic.

In September 1966 the three crews selected to represent the RAF in the year's SAC Bombing Competition (this year code named Big Flight) flew to Fairchild Air Force Base, Spokane, Washington: they were Wing Commander D A Arnott and crew and Flight Lieutenant B K McLaren as reserve; the detachment commander was Cottesmore's Station Commander Group Captain J Garden DFC. The competition had by this time developed into a sophisticated test of all aspects of the bomber crew's skill; high level night navigation, high level bombing, low level navigation and bombing (Hi-Lo-Hi profiles) and later flight refuelling all in competition with SAC's best crews. Out of 40 competing crews the final Cottesmore crew placings were:

Captain	Navigation	Bombing	Combined Navigation and Bombing
Arnott	5th	30th	24th
Crowder	16th	24th	21st
Downs	24th	37th	36th

At home, Cottesmore aircraft continued with their main role commitments. 1967 was liberally sprinkled with Exercise Kinsmans, the object of which was to exercise the Medium Bomber Force facilities at a variety of dispersal airfields such as Leeming, Yeovilton, Ballykelly and RRE Pershore. There were further Kinsmans to Leuchars, Leconfield and Lyneham. There were numerous Groupexes mostly of the Exercise Billion variety, and between 7 and 17 March the Station participated in the annual Bomber Command Inter-Squadron Competition. 9 Squadron achieved an encouraging degree of success in this competition coming 2nd in the Bombing and Navigation sections for the Laurence Minot Trophy, 4th in the Communications section, 3rd in the Navigation section and 2nd in the Free Fall Bombing section.

On 6 June 1967 the first of a series of 'Westabout' Pacific Rangers departed Cottesmore when Flight Lieutenant Gillanders and Flight Lieutenant Mitchell flew west to Goose Bay, Offutt, McClennan Air Force Base (Sacramento in California), Honolulu, Wake Island, Guam, Tengah, Gan, Muharraq (Bahrain in the Persian Gulf) and Akrotiri and on to Cottesmore.

Two Crew Chiefs were taken in each aircraft and a pannier in the bomb bay laden with spare wheels, brake parachutes, other items that experience had shown to be useful, and the crews' luggage. The Crew Chiefs spent the flight sitting in some discomfort, encumbered by heavy parachute and survival packs and in semi-darkness relieved only by the glow from the radar. They sat on the steps facing inward, below the level of the rear crew members, who were themselves below the level of the pilots. It was only possible to see out of the aircraft by drawing the blackout blind behind the pilots and climbing, and standing on the ladder between them, or by stepping down from their seat onto the visual bomb aimers position in the nose. Both actions required a fair amount of physical effort. Normally, they elected to stay where they were. At the end of each leg they fitted a new tail parachute, folded and stored the used one, fitted the blanks in the engine intakes, covered the wheels and if there were unserviceabilities, they fixed them and finally supervised the refuelling. They were great and uncomplaining men, skilful and fiercely protective of their aircraft and prepared to work long hours to ensure that the crews maintained their planned itinerary.

1967 was the year of 12 Squadron's disbandment but until the official closure at 2359 hours on 31 December 1967 they were busy on the full range of training activities: Lone Rangers; Goose Rangers where low flying exercises were carried out over the wild Canadian Arctic; Desert low flying using the El Adem low level route; Western Rangers; Kinsmans, Co-ops, Billions, trials, scrambles and Sunspots. On 12 June 1967, a Vulcan took off on a special flight to photograph two bridges over the Albert Canal at Veldwezelt and Vroenhoven. It was here, on 12 May 1940, that five 12 Squadron crews from Amifontaine volunteered to answer a desperate appeal from the Belgian authorities to slow the German advance by attacking the heavily defended bridges. All five Battles were shot down in the attempt.

As a climax to their tour on 12 Squadron, the CO, Wing Commander Tew and crew carried out a 'Westabout' Pacific Ranger between 9 and 23 October following the now familiar Vulcan route, the

Vulcans of 35 Squadron at Malta in 1968 during a 'Sunspot' detachment. *(Photo: MoD).*

Throughout much of this time Cottesmore maintained a Station Flight to ferry men and equipment around the country. *Above:* An Avro Anson C19 at Odiham in 1961. *Below:* an ex-Cottesmore Station Flight de Havilland Canada Chipmunk, used to give Air Cadets flying experience, seen here in 1990 with the EFTS at Swinderby. *(Photo: MoD)*

'newest' part of which: from Honolulu (Pearl Harbour) to Wake Island, Guam to Singapore were all famous in history as the bases hit simultaneously by Japan on 7 December 1941 (the 8th for Wake Island, Guam and Singapore on the western side of the international date line) which brought America into the war against Japan and Germany.

When 12 Squadron disbanded, some B2s were flown to Waddington to join 44, 50 and 101 squadrons where they replaced the last few remaining Vulcan B1As. On 1 October 1969, the Squadron reformed with Buccaneer S2s at Honington in the Maritime Strike role. There were other changes in this significant year. On 30 April 1968 Bomber and Fighter Commands combined to form Strike Command (STC) with Air Chief Marshal Sir Wallace Kyle as C-in-C, and the remainder of the V-Force, now consisting of Vulcans and Victors, came under 1 (Bomber) Group at Bawtry in Yorkshire.

Vulcan weaknesses.
An accident at Cottesmore, on 30 June 1968, illustrated one of the design limitations of the Vulcan which made the rear crew members vulnerable when flying at low level. All three of the V-Bombers, Vulcan, Victor and Valiant, had been designed with ejection seats for the pilots but not for the rear crew. When forced to abandon the aircraft the Vulcan Navs, AEO and Crew Chief left by sliding down the door which opened downwards against the slipstream - if there was time and altitude to spare. If the undercarriage was down the escaping crew were faced by a very solid looking nose wheel oleo.

35 Squadron Vulcans at Gan on 29 April 1965. *(Photo: MoD)*

Vulcan XM604 suffered a fire in number two engine during an overshoot at Cottesmore. This led rapidly to a bomb bay fire and severe damage to the flying controls. The captain, Flight Lieutenant P Tait, ordered his crew to abandon the aircraft as he found the aircraft increasingly unresponsive to the controls. The co-pilot, Flying Officer M Gillett suffered a broken arm but ejected safely. Tait delayed his own departure until the last possible second to give his rear crew a chance, but after the aircraft had rolled agonisingly slowly into a steep nose down attitude, he went, and was only saved when his deploying chute was caught in some high power cables retarding his fall. His gallant action was unable to prevent the death of Flying Officer B D Goodman (Nav radar), Flight Lieutenant S R Sumpter (Nav Plotter), Flying Officer M J Whelan (AEO) and Flight Lieutenant A W Bennett (Screen Nav radar). Major retrospective modification of the escape system was considered but was rejected as too complex and time consuming for the aircraft to be spared from front line activities, although minor improvements such as swivel seats and quick disconnect personal equipment had been made.

Other changes were in the air. The British Government was having another of its 'long hard looks' at defence expenditure, commitments and resources. From June 1968 the QRA was borne exclusively by the Vulcan squadrons as the two Victor Blue Steel squadrons were disbanded. There were new commitments to fulfil to the Central Treaty Organisation (CENTO) composed of Iran, Pakistan, Turkey, USA and Britain, on the southern flank of NATO which Cottesmore aircraft would carry out. But before they did so, there was the 50th Anniversary of the RAF to celebrate. On 14 June 1968, Cottesmore Vulcans formed part of the fly past for the Royal Review of the RAF at Abingdon and again the following day for the public. As part of the celebrations, Cottesmore was opened to the public on a 'Good Neighbour's Day'. The celebrations continued overseas when the Maryland National Air Races were dedicated to the RAF's 50th anniversary. Two Vulcans flew to Andrews AFB in Washington for flying displays at Frederick AFB Maryland on 5th, 6th and 7th July.

The Sunspot Detachments of September and October 1968 were preambles to more permanent moves eastwards by the Cottesmore squadrons. The task was to re-inforce the Near East Air Force (NEAF) during times of tension in the conventional role and the Sunspot was to give them experience of this. Two aircraft left for Luqa (Malta) on 27 September followed shortly afterwards by a further six supported by personnel and equipment flown out in a Lockheed C-130 Hercules and four Hawker Siddeley Argosies. Crews embarked on a training schedule which included low and medium level bombing on the El Adem range in Libya and high and low level navigation exercises over the Libyan and Calabrian low level routes in Italy.

The Cottesmore Wing began a more permanent move to Akrotiri, Cyprus, on 15 January 1969 when the first wave of four 35 Squadron crews took off from Cottesmore supported at intervals by 20

84

Cottesmore Wing Vulcan B2 XM647 - circa 1969 *(Photo: MoD)*

Hercules and Britannias of Air Support Command (ASC) carrying equipment and ground personnel. Wing Commander Carver led the way in XH562.

The last QRA duty was carried out by a Cottesmore aircraft on 31 January 1969, (although Vulcans elsewhere continued the commitment until 30 June). Group Captain W J H Roberts marked the occasion with the following letter to his OC Eng Wing, Wing Commander A G White.

"Dear Alan

Todays sees the start of the last day of QRA at Cottesmore. This is the last of 1,551 consecutive days of QRA by the Vulcans here alone. As you are well aware this has been a vital responsibility calling for the highest standards of sense of duty and attention to detail. I congratulate you and all those of your Wing who have played such an important part in this achievement. I would be glad if you would pass on my congratulations to your personnel and particularly to Line Servicing Squadron and Armament Engineering Squadron".

Mr Dennis Healey, the Minister of Defence, later paid his own tribute in the House of Commons
To the way in which the officers and men concerned at all levels in the Royal Air Force have discharged their arduous responsibilities over the last 12 years.

The C-in-C STC Sir Denis Spotswood, received the following signal from Sir John Grandy, a former C-in-C Bomber Command:
'maintaining, at all times throughout seven years, the highest state of readiness which the ROYAL AIR FORCE had known in peacetime. The way in which QRA has been performed

and the reaction of the force to the operational demands of our plans and those of SACEUR has been an unsurpassed demonstration of professional skill, dedication and tenacity. The long hours of arduous duty in cockpits, crew rooms, dispersal, hangars and operations rooms have brought the reward of knowing that a vital task has been successfully completed.'

The second wave of Cottesmore aircraft to complete 35 Squadrons move, left on 5 February. The first echelon of 9 Squadron crews followed on 26 February. With the fourth wave on 9 March the final departure of the Vulcan from Cottesmore was complete. It was an occasion to remember. They chose to go with a roar rather than a whimper with a scramble take-off initiated by the Bomber Controller from Strike Command Operations Centre. It was a day of freezing fog as wives and families gathered at a special enclosure erected beside the Operational Readiness Platform to listen to the pipes and drums of 1 Group pipe band until the noise of the 16 Bristol Olympus engines in close proximity drowned all else. The neighbours also noticed that something was afoot as the Bomber Controller scrambled the four aircraft. They roared down the Cottesmore runway for the last time, lifted off and turned to a south easterly heading. On the airfield as the sound of engines faded, the wailing lament of the pipers could be heard again as they stood in the mist like disconsolate chimeras. Just over four hours later the aircraft touched down at Akrotiri and the NEAF Bomber Wing was in business. Canberras, Argosies and Vickers Varsities of 115 Squadron began arriving to replace the Vulcan in April 1969.

Departure of the last Vulcan, 35 Squadron, from
Cottesmore to Akrotiri on 9 March 1969. *(Photo: MoD)*

CHAPTER SIX

90 Signals Group and the return of the Canberra.

On 1 April 1969, three weeks after the last Vulcans had left Cottesmore, the advance party of 115 Squadron arrived from Watton to prepare the way for its Varsities and Argosies, which arrived on 18 April. The change of aircraft and role meant a change of Group from 1 Group to 90 (Signals) Group. Three Canberra units followed: 360 Squadron on 21 April, with their T17 ECM Canberras and 98 Squadron, on 17 April, with B2s, E15s (modified B15 bombers) and T4 dual control trainers, also from Watton where they had spent the last 5 years. On 19 May, 231 OCU flew in from Bassingbourne with their Canberra B2s and T4s where they had operated for considerably longer. On 30 May Group Captain L G A Bastard AFC took command of Cottesmore from Group Captain Roberts and reported that he had 56 aircraft on strength comprising of six different types: Varsities, Argosies, and Canberra B2s, Canberra T4s, E15s and T17s.

Canberra B2 WJ681 of 231 OCU in 1975 *(Photo: MAP)*

The Varsities had been flying with the RAF since entering Service in October 1951 with 201 AFS at Swinderby. This reliable and popular aircraft had been used in a variety of roles including a conversion trainer for pilots going on to heavy piston engined aircraft, as an advanced instructional aircraft for navigators and bomb aimers and in its role with 115 Squadron as a calibrator of airfield aids. Powered by two 1,950 hp Bristol Hercules engines, it had a good range, plenty of power and an agreeable amount of space for the crew to move around in. Its career ended in May 1976 at 6 FTS at Finningley when it was superseded by the Jetstream.

The Argosy was the second aircraft of that name produced by the Armstrong Whitworth Company, who later became part of the Hawker Siddeley Group. The first was a 3 engined bi-plane powered by 385 hp direct drive Jaguar engines with accommodation for 20 passengers in wicker seats. The second aircraft and the one used by 115 Squadron was a four engined Rolls-Royce Dart turbo prop aircraft with twin booms and a central fuselage, originally designed to carry 83 passengers or freight or a combination of both. The aircraft was designed as a private venture, even if the makers did have a covetous eye on the military market. They were justified. The Air Ministry placed an order for 20 aircraft in 1959 and later increased it to 56. Modifications for RAF requirements included a more robust floor, suitable for heavy vehicles and hydraulically operated doors hingeing upwards and downwards at the rear of the fuselage (rather than the sideways opening doors for the airlines). The doors were capable of being operated in flight for use by paratroops; the wing was also strengthened and provision made for a greater fuel load. The aircraft looked right, the twin-boom arrangement offered a clean uncluttered fuselage for the easy handling of bulky cargo, it was versatile, the engines were well tried,

Argosy E1 of 115 Squadron gets airborne *(Photo: MAP)*

reliable and easy to maintain and it was popular with passengers and aircrew. It should have been a successful aircraft, but the plain fact of the matter was that it had a disappointing climb performance and a comparitively low speed; this signalled its early demise. It lasted only 10 years before it was replaced by a world wide winner - the C-130 Hercules.

The first squadron to operate the Argosy was 114 at Benson, followed by 105 Squadron which moved to Khormaksar, in Aden, while 215 Squadron's Argosies operated from Changi, Singapore, from August 1963. When the RAF commitments to the Middle and Far East began to be reduced in 1969, 215 Squadron was disbanded, and many of its crews and aircraft went to 70 Squadron at Akrotiri. 105 Squadron was moved from Aden to Muharraq where its aircraft were used to maintain supplies from Bahrain to the Gulf Stations of Sharjah, Masirah and Salalah and to support the British and Allied Forces in the Gulf. The Argosy did well in these circumstances, the stage lengths of 300 to 500 miles permitted the full payload capacity to be used. As the commitment was reduced some of the aircraft were withdrawn and transferred to 115 Squadron at Watton. Here they were modified for signals duties, mainly for the calibration of airfield approach and landing and radio aids; the aircraft remained in that role at Cottesmore.

This was the second occupation of Cottesmore by Canberras, the first had been nearly 15 years earlier. It is a long time in the life of an aircraft but since then much had happened to this versatile aircraft. It had seen brief but spirited action in the Near East, a much longer action against Communist forces in Malaya and Indonesian forces in Malaysia, and had fully proved its value.

By 1969 there were at least 13 versions of the Canberra in the RAF. The B2 and B6 bombers, three types of photographic reconnaissance aircraft (PR3, PR7 and PR9), the T4 dual control trainer, the B(I)8 bomber intruder, the T11 and T19 AI radar operated trainers, the B15 and B16 tactical nuclear or conventional bombers and ground attack aircraft, T17 ECM aircraft and the TT18 target tower. The intruder or interdicter Canberra employed a spectacular though dangerous and often inaccurate method of weapon delivery known as the low altitude bombing system (LABS) technique. This entailed an approach to the target at low-level and high speed before pulling up into a half loop to roll out on to a reciprocal heading. The bomb was released at a precomputed release angle during the pull up. As well as its aerobatic capability the aircraft could be rapidly converted to other roles with gun packs fitted underneath the fuselage for close support and ground attack work.

Canberra B2 of 98 Squadron, wearing the 90 Signals group titles on the upper fuselage in 1971 *(Photo: MoD)*

Airfield and Navigation Aid Calibration.

98 Squadron had a less spectacular though important role to play, similar to 115 Squadron's, namely calibrating all RAF navigational and airfield approach aids worldwide, and since stronger links were being forged with Europe, this extended to NATO airfields. One such detachment was to Cameri and Treviso in the northern part of Italy, where 2 aircraft supported by 11 engineers spent 3 weeks calibrating NATO airfields in the area.

360 Squadron was a unique joint RAF/RN squadron with 25% of its personnel sailors, and from September 1973, every fourth CO was a RN Commander. It was formed by combining 97 Squadron RAF and 831 Naval Air Squadron. The Squadron worked closely with a range of services including the Royal Navy. Shortly after its arrival at Cottesmore, aircraft of the Squadron were detached to Brawdy in May 1969 to provide ECM training for HMS Eagle during her work up.

231 OCU had been responsible for training Canberra crews since it received its first B2 in February 1952, at that time the only jet-bomber conversion unit in the world. Its role developed as time went by, in 1958 photographic reconnaissance training was started and in 1961 a low-level syllabus was introduced, but by the time the unit reached Cottesmore its main task was the conversion training of aircrew onto the Canberra, while the operational aspects became the responsibility of the squadrons to which the crews were posted.

One of the first decisions made by the squadrons after their arrival at Cottesmore was that the centralised servicing system which was the accepted norm, would simply not do for them. The main reason given was that the layout of the airfield required the four units to use dispersals on both sides of the airfield. The CO of 360 Squadron, Wing Commander R M Dubock AFC, proposed to make the units semi-autonomous by giving them a first line servicing flight under the command of OC Engineering Wing but under the operational control of the squadron commanders. This would of course require more servicing manpower when the first line element was established. One of the main advantages cited by the proposal was the great boost to morale which the new arrangement would give to the squadron groundcrews. It is interesting to compare the reasons for the original proposals for the Victors to change to the central servicing system, and those of the Canberra squadrons which wished to revert to the squadron system. In doing so it should be borne in mind that there were only two Victor squadrons at Cottesmore at the time.

The widely spaced squadron dispersals posed other problems which largely revolved round the lack of MT and drivers. At Watton, crews had been able to walk to their aircraft from the squadron accommodation which was sited nearby. At Cottesmore, aircrew took over the driving and for several of the early months, lack of manpower and the number of squadron detachments adversely affected the accomplishment of some of the monthly tasks. However the manpower situation slowly improved, as did the monthly achievement.

One of 98 Squadron's early detachments in June 1969, was when Flight Lieutenant Woodhouse departed on Exercise Safari 6, in WH911, to flight check aids in the Mediterranean, Persian Gulf and the Far East. Squadron Leader Landeryou, the Squadron Commander, and Flight Lieutenant J Simmons left the UK later in the month by ASC VC10 to relieve them at Butterworth. It was during this month that the two signals squadrons took over the responsibility for checking Royal Navy radars, the first of which, at Yeovilton, was checked on 12 June. At the end of June, 115 Squadron reported that its aircraft had checked 26 ILS, 16 PAR, 5 ACR7, 1 MPN11, 4 CPN4, 13 TACAN, 10 CADF, 1 CRDF and 6 Eurekas.

At the end of March 1970, GEE, that excellent navigational aid for all aircraft flying over, or in the vicinity of the United Kingdom, was withdrawn from service and the Canberras were re-equipped with TACAN and SSR1520. Both these aids gave the aircraft much more flexibility in carrying out their increasingly world wide tasks. During their time at Cottesmore there were a number of exercises with the fleet in several locations: there were detachments to Bodo, Bardufoss, Stavangar and Oslo in Norway, Luqa (Malta), Akrotiri, Muharraq and the Gulf States, Iran, Gibraltar, Butterworth and Singapore (Changi and Tengah), Italy, Germany, and Lajes via Monte Real.

On 29 January 1971, a 360 Squadron Canberra T4 (WJ862) and a T17 (WH874) were involved in a mid air collision during a formation flying exercise near Mansfield. All five of the crew members ejected from their aircraft safely and were picked up with only minor injuries. There were two other Canberra incidents, involving 231 OCU aircraft during this their second term at Cottesmore. The first,

WH874, a Canberra T17 of 360 Squadron banks away from the camera aircraft in 1971.
(Photo: MoD)

on 12 March 1973, ended happily when a student, Flying Officer A Miller, experienced technical difficulties with both engines during a night exercise. As a precautionary measure, the navigator Flight Lieutenant R E Pocock was ordered to eject. He suffered minor injuries but was able to use his survival equipment, to activate the Sarbe and the mini flares to attract the attention of a USAF search helicopter from Alconbury. Flying Officer Miller managed to land the aircraft safely.

The second incident, on 2 August, had a less happy end. It happened during night flying after a day of heat and haze. At 2300 hrs, Canberra B2 WJ674 was seen to pass over the Fox Inn on the A1 in flames. Onlookers saw the navigator, Flight Lieutenant Murray (now Squadron Leader Murray in the groundschool of the TTTE), eject during the approach to the airfield. They saw his parachute deploy just before he hit the newly ploughed field behind the pub where helping hands were almost immediately on the scene. Unfortunately, the pilot, Flight Lieutenant Dennis, left his ejection too late for his parachute to completely deploy and he was killed.

A Vickers Varsity of 115 Squadron. *(Photo: Sqn Ldr C.P. Russell-Smith)*

On 12 February 1971, 115 Squadron's last Varsity (WJ911) was retired, after having received its first one on 21 August 1958. On 19 May 1971 a 115 Squadron Argosy featured in an unusual but rewarding incident. The crew were engaged on an ILS flight check at St Mawgan when after about ninety minutes (and well into their task), they heard a Canberra reporting a disturbed patch of sea some 20 miles west of Trevose Head. ATC St Mawgan asked the Argosy to investigate. While heading for the position they heard the Canberra crew report that they were receiving transmissions from two Sarbe distress beacons. The Argosy took over the search from the Canberra which returned to St Mawgan, and assumed control to direct operations at the scene. Using Violet Picture, they located the general position of the survivors and directed two Sea Vixens from Yeovilton and two helicopters from Chivenor and Culdrose to the scene. The Argosy searched at 1,500 feet, one of the Sea Vixens at 500 feet and the other at 6,000 feet. Ten minutes after beginning their search the Argosy crew spotted the first survivor and shortly afterwards, the second, both safely in their dinghies. The Argosy circled continuously passing the position to St Mawgan and the approaching helicopters and then pinpointed the dinghies to the helicopters when they arrived. Both men were winched to safety and taken to St Mawgan where they were able to give a full account of their Phantom aircraft's crash. The Argosy returned to complete its flight check at St Mawgan.

Airframes and Units come of age.

Some of the aircraft in the Cottesmore squadrons were vintage specimens. On 9 October 1972 Canberra T4 WD944, flown by 98 Squadron, became the first Canberra to complete 21 years service with the RAF. It was originally a B2 allotted to 101 Squadron at Binbrook in 1951, but in May 1954 it was damaged in a wheels-up landing. After repair and refurbishing it was put into store at 15 Maintenance Unit (MU) at Wroughton until June 1956 when it was converted to a T4 and allocated to the Central Flying School at Little Rissington. After further modifications WD944 went to Laarbruch and then Wildenrath where it was used in the Station flight for training purposes. 98 Squadron received the aircraft on 9 October 1967 at Watton. WD955, which joined 360 Squadron, was also from the original batch but had undergone major modifications to become a T17.

It was also in October 1972 that Canberra PR7 WH791 was brought to Cottesmore and erected on blocks just inside the main gate. It was not one of the types actually used at Cottesmore but as no B2s were available a PR7 was deemed to be near enough, and in fact the number first painted on the aircraft at Cottesmore was WH717 which had been  the number of one of 44 Squadron's aircraft at Cottesmore in 1954. It was later changed back to its true number. It had been built by English Electric at Preston and delivered to Bomber Command Acceptance and Modifications Unit at Lindholme in May 1954. From there it went to 542 Squadron at Wyton. In February 1955 it was given a specialist fit and went to 82 Squadron at Wyton. From 1 September 1956 until July 1960 it served with 58 Squadron at Wyton where it took part in Far East Photographic Survey Operations. After spells with various MUs it was issued to the FEAF and until the end of its operational career on 16 January 1970 it served with 81 Squadron at Tengah.

STC economy measures of 1 January 1972 announced decreases in establishment for several squadrons including 98 Squadron whose eight Canberra E15s and two Canberra T4s were reduced to six EI5s and one T4. Aircrew were reduced from the CO, 12 pilots and 12 navigators to the CO, 7 pilots and 8 navigators and the groundcrew from 58 to 44. The task was also considerably reduced, involving the loss of virtually all flight checking tasks in the Mediterranean area. At the same time, 115 Squadron reported that its ground- crew were 69% under establishment as Argosy XP448 returned to base after completing the calibration of the VOR and DME at Seychelles Civil Airport and other routine calibration tasks at Gan, Masirah and Akrotiri. Power was also in short

On 9 November 1972, Canberra T4 WD944 'came of age' when it became the first Canberra to complete 21 years of service with the RAF. The aircraft carries the Squadron badge of 'Cerberus, the three-headed watchdog at the gates of Hades. *(Photo: MoD)*

supply in February 1972, as strikes by coal miners caused nationwide power cuts. Some erstwhile clients cancelled flight checks on their airfield equipment for this reason.

231 OCU, at the time under the command of Squadron Leader Merriman, celebrated 21 years of continuous operations with Canberras on 21 February 1973. The Unit had become 231 OCU in 1947, when it was training light bomber and marker crews with Mosquito BXVIs at Coningsby. It was disbanded at Hemswell when the Mosquito retired from its role as a bomber, and was reformed at Bassingbourne in October 1951 where it embraced several tasks including Mosquito training with Mosquito PR34s for long range reconnaissance training and Mosquito T3s for conversion to the Hornets of FEAF. It also had Meteor T7s and PR10s for reconnaissance training and Ansons and Tiger Moths for communications. The first Canberra arrived in February 1952. The unit's long association with Bomber and Strike Command well justifying its proud motto: 'Prepared to Attack'.

For the first time since 1965, Cottesmore was one of the six RAF stations opened to the public for Battle of Britain displays in September 1973. There was some concern expressed before the event that little of the expertise gained in organising previous shows remained, but the planning was meticulous and the event was very successful. It included participation by several NATO countries including RCAF, USAF, Norwegian Air Force and 12 Fouga Magisters of the Patrouille de France who gave a brilliant formation display. This inspired a wag in the October edition of the Station Magazine, the Clarion, to annotate a photograph of the team trailing smoke: 'Leader au number huit. Vous avey let votre gar out - Merde!' All proceeds from the days activities were donated to the RAF Benevolent Fund, the RAF Association and the RAF Museum. One of the fund raising activities was the raffle of an Austin Allegro car. The winner was Mr R J Payne who received the car keys from the Station Commander, Group Captain A F Jenkins CVO, after it had been driven from the cavernous hold of an Argosy.

28 September 1973 was an important occasion for 360 Squadron. The C-in-C STC, Air Chief Marshal Sir Andrew Humphrey KCB OBE DFC AFC presented Commander G Oxley RN, the first naval officer to command the Squadron, with its well chosen Badge featuring the Druce Moth (Melese Laodamia Druce) superimposed on the trident with the motto 'CONFUNDEMUS', implying: we shall throw into confusion. The Druce Moth is a favourite prey of the bat. When attacked, the moth listens out for the bat's emissions and produces a jamming signal which confuses its enemy long enough to effect an escape. The trident referred to the naval connection.

Effects of the three day week.

January and February 1974 saw the introduction, in the face of another miner's strike, of the three day working week and the fuel economy campaign. Cottesmore achieved some remarkable savings. The allocated target figures and the actual consumption of the various fuels with the percentage savings are herewith demonstrated:

Aviation Fuel	445,300 galls	311,552 galls	69.5%
Civgas	3,570 galls	2,965 galls	82.5%
Diesel	1,020 galls	1,142 galls	112.5%
Furnace Fuel Oil	88,555 galls	67,430 galls	81%

The target saving for electricity was 10%. In fact the total consumption of 417,930 Kwh works out at 13,482 Kwh per day compared with 24,600 Kwh per day in 1973 - a percentage saving of 45%. The hours flown by the squadron were proportionately curtailed until March when the restrictions were partially lifted after the General Election.

25 years of the Canberra.

The 25th Anniversary of the first Canberra flight was celebrated on 22 May 1974 at Cottesmore, at that time looked upon as the home of the Canberra (bringing back memories of 15, 44, 57 and 149 squadrons in the early 50s when Bomber Command had 408 Canberras operational in the United Kingdom). Roland Beamont was the guest of honour. Apart from the early testing of the aircraft he had also broken several of the 22 World Records achieved by it as had others of the distinguished guests that day, amongst whom were Marshal of the Royal Air Force Sir Dermot Boyle, Air Chief Marshal Sir Lewis Hodges, Air Marshal Sir John Whitley and Air Vice-Marshal Ivor Broom. Twelve different variants of the Canberra were assembled on display: a B2 (WJ603) came from 85 Squadron, a PR3 (WE146) came from Llanbedr, 98 Squadron contributed a T4 (WD944) and an E15 (WH948), a B6 (WK163) came from RRE Pershore (the same aircraft that had established an altitude record of 70,310 feet on 28 August 1957 with a Napier Scorpion engine fitted), 13 Squadron sent a PR7 (WT530) and 39 Squadron a PR9 (XH170), the T17 (WJ633) was a 360 Squadron aircraft and a TT18 (WJ721) came from 7 Squadron and a T19 (WH903) from 100 Squadron. A T22 (WH801) came from FRADU and a SC9 (XH132, a one-off special version of a PR9) came from Pershore. After a flying display a reunion dinner for the people associated with the aircraft rounded off the day.

The British Government conducted one of its periodic defence reviews in 1975; this one was more comprehensive than most. It announced the closure of 12 RAF Stations and the reduction of Cottesmore to a state of care and maintenance. 360 Squadron was the first to go on 5 August 1975, to Wyton. It is still operating from there and seems likely to do so for some time. The 40th anniversary of the Canberra was celebrated there on another memorable occasion on 13 May 1989. 231 OCU moved to Marham on 18 February 1976 and 98 Squadron was disbanded on 27 February; its standard lies in Cottesmore's village church of Saint Nicholas. It can still be seen there in the Air Force Memorial Chapel dedicated to airmen from many countries who lost their lives flying from Cottesmore.

The Argosies of 115 Squadron departed for Brize Norton, on 23 February, where they survived for a further 2 years. On 24 January 1978, Squadron Leader F Hayward flew Argosy XR143 back to Cottesmore on its last operational sortie. The RAF's free fall parachute team, the Falcons, jumped from the aircraft over the airfield before it carried out its final duty; the calibration of the station approach aids.

The chapter was almost complete but it was not quite the end of the Canberra at Cottesmore. Its venerable age had begun to catch up with it, and some of the gyrations that the old lady had been called upon to perform had induced some Cat 3 airframe problems. 71 MU and a contractors working party moved into Cottesmore to rectify the faults. Work continued in the hangars long after the airfield had been handed over to Care and Maintenance on 31 March 1976.

An aerial view of the Canberra static display on 22 May 1974 on the occasion of the 25th Anniversary of the first Canberra flight. *(Photo: P H T Green)*

CHAPTER SEVEN

Enter the Tornado!.

Tornado GR1 (B-55, ZA359) in 67 degree wing sweep with full afterburner.
(Photo: P.A. Jackson)

Europeans could now look back on a continent that had started the century full of hope, more powerful than ever before but had then seen it tear itself apart in two terrible conflicts. From the devastation they witnessed the growth of a hopeful idea; the idea of a cooperating Europe. Two visionary Frenchmen, Robert Schumann and Jean Monnet, led the way with the idea of a United Europe. Robert Schumann came from Alsace on the border between France and Germany. As a German citizen in 1914 he had fought in the German Army against France. The Treaty of Versailles made him a Frenchman and in 1939 he found himself fighting for France against Germany. After the war he became Prime Minister of France and with economist Jean Monnet, and the enthusiastic support of Chancellor Konrad Adenauer of Germany, they started the European Coal and Steel Community. Holland, Belgium and Luxembourg joined economically to form the Benelux Union and in 1957 the process continued when the Treaty of Rome created the European Economic Community of France, Germany, Italy and the Benelux countries. In January 1972 Britain, led by the Prime Minister Mr Edward Heath, joined and a year later Denmark and Ireland followed, and now Spain, Portugal and Greece are part of it. Austria has applied and with the recent sweeping upheavals in Eastern Europe, goodness knows what will follow. Cooperation is in the air. Cooperation was in the air in a smaller way in the late 60s and 70s when Italy, West Germany and Britain got together to design and build the Multi Role Combat Aircraft (MRCA), later named the Tornado.

The Euronational Company of Panavia was formed on 26 March 1969 in München, West Germany, comprising Aeritalia of Napoli, British Aerospace of Warton and Messerschmitt-Bölkow-Blohm (MBB) of München; work on the Turbo-Union RB199 engine for the Tornado was also shared between the three countries: Fiat of Italy, MTU of Germany and Rolls-Royce. The Director of Flight Operations was the uniquely qualified Roland Beamont with his unrivalled experience with the Canberra, Lightning and short lived but revolutionary TSR2.

This was not the first time that the three countries had successfully collaborated in aviation matters. In the mid 1950s a requirement for a NATO Light Tactical Strike Fighter was identified. In a competition between Dassault (the Etendard), Breguet (the Taon) and Nord, who subsequently dropped out (all of France), and Fiat with the G91 of Italy, all chose the British lightweight Orpheus turbo jet to power their aircraft. The Fiat G91 under the brilliant direction of the Company's Technical Director, Guiseppe Gabrielli, easily won the competition on merit. The aircraft was built in large

numbers in Italy and Germany and the Orpheus 803 designed by Stanley Hooker, rated at 5,000lbs of thrust was built by Fiat in Italy and Kloeckner-Humbolt-Deutz (KHD) in West Germany. The aircraft proved to be very popular and had a long and successful career. The whole enterprise was largely funded by the American Mutual Weapons Development Programme (MWDP) generously masterminded by Col. Johnny Driscoll USAF and was the inspiration for the emerging European Aircraft Industry.

But European cooperation in aviation ideas goes back much further into mists of time - 500 years in fact to Leonardo da Vinci. In his autobiography 'Not Much Of An Engineer', Stanley Hooker records that after his break with Rolls-Royce in 1949 when he was working on the Bristol Olympus engine which powered the Vulcan and the Bristol Pegasus which powered the Harrier, the Bristol engineers took up one of da Vinci's ideas. They abandoned forged blades for the HP turbines on these engines and instead cast their blades using da Vinci's lost wax process to produce precisely repeated sculptures. When Bristol Siddeley Engines Ltd. were taken over by Rolls-Royce in 1966, Rolls were still using forged blades in Nimonic high nickel alloy and having enormous problems with their Conway by pass engine which powered the Victor 2 and VC10 and the emerging RB211. The Bristol/da Vinci ideas were successfully adapted to suit these engines and ultimately, since engines are derivative, the RB199 for the Tornado.

The Tornado was conceived so that, as near as possible, all the qualities necessary for a multi role combat aircraft were combined in one aircraft. This was done with the introduction of the first European variable geometry wing to give short take-off and landing and long loiter times (when fully extended), and high speed (when fully swept) in low level flight, a three spool bypass reheated turbofan engine for short take-off and long range at low level, and an integrated avionics system to give it an all weather capability.

The Tornado is the first fighter bomber with comfortable handling qualities in all areas of flight and in all weather conditions. It is also Europe's first fly-by-wire aircraft, with manual reversion available in the unlikely event of complete failure of the computerised flight control system. The sophisticated autopilot and flight director system permits hands-off flight in any weather conditions, down to a height of 200 ft at speeds up to 0.9 Mach. There are no unpleasant surprises in the extremely wide flight envelope, which matches that of the F-104G Starfighter at high speed, while the full-span manoeuvre flaps and high thrust/weight ratio permit Hawk-like turning performance at low speed. Built-in system redundancy takes the sting out of most in-flight emergencies, and the aircraft retains its easy flying characteristics even after failure of major systems. The Tornado is also a first-class navigators' aeroplane, as its operational success depends on the efficiency with which he handles the radar, navigation, weapons and ECM equipment. Very close crew co-operation is vital to get the best out of the aircraft and its systems.

The Tornado forms the backbone of Western European Air Power and will do so until well into the 21st Century. The original numbers of aircraft planned were: 385 for the RAF (including 165 of the Air Defence Variant), 212 for the German Air Force, 112 for the German Navy and 100 for the Italian Air Force. There are now substantial follow-on orders. The training task for the Tri-National Tornado Training Establishment (TTTE) has, therefore, been geared to produce about 300 aircrew per year. To meet this task the TTTE currently maintains a mix of British, German and Italian aircraft, and two flight simulators. The TTTE Ground School staff consists of 10 pilots and 10 navigators and the flying instructional staff, 38 pilots and 18 navigators. The numbers of aircraft and instructors represent the proportion of financial investment by the countries involved.

The Tri-national Tornado Training Establisment.

The first Tornado prototype D-9591 made its maiden flight from Manching on 14 August 1974; the second, XX946, flew from Warton on 30 October 1974 and the third, XX947, a dual control trainer, from Warton on 5 August 1975. Meanwhile, a Joint Operational Training Study Group was set up to look into the possibility of combining some of the training. They reported in March 1975 recommending the use of Cottesmore. The Tri-National memorandum of Understanding, which confirmed the creation of the TTTE, was signed on 8 May 1979.

There were many enthusiastic speeches of support for the idea; Sir Arthur Hockaday spoke of the advantages the collaboration would bring; each country would learn from the others. Statssekretar Dr Hiehle of Germany and The Honourable Giuseppe Caroli of Italy agreed: 'We all benefit, there are

Two Tornadoes from British Aerospace Warton overfly Cottesmore on 8 May 1979 during the signing of the undertaking to establish the TTTE *(Photo: MoD)*

advantages not only of a technical and financial nature but also of mutual understanding and strengthened ties of friendship'. The Chief of Staff of the Italian Air Force described the TTTE as the most tangible witness of common will stimulating the NATO Air Forces. Other spokesmen mentioned the German qualities of organisation and discipline, Italian flair and British flexibility. One of the first things that visitors to the Cottesmore community notice is that there are no national characteristics only an immense good will between the three nations.

Cottesmore was transferred from Care and Maintenance to Active State on 1 April 1978 with Wing Commander B N Wanstall as Station Commander. Shortly afterwards the Tornado Aircrew Course Design Team (TACDT) moved from HQSTC to Cottesmore under the command of Wing Commander Oakden, and since construction work was continuing apace, they took up residence in the Officers' Mess. Their business was to create the training syllabus for the aircrew to meet the objectives of the three Air Forces and the German Navy. The Wing Commander's team consisted of Squadron Leader Nunn, Major Volk, Major Dombrove, Maggiore Pollice, Major Hoeffer, Major von Knobloch, Squadron Leader Hartnett, Corporal Marshall and Mrs Hester Brown who still works for the TTTE and who supplied many of the early facts about the TTTE.

The Tornado Ground Servicing School, now known as the Tornado Maintenance School (TMS), was the next to arrive. It was officially opened by Air Vice-Marshal P Bairsto on 31 October 1979 although training had already started on 22 October. This was an independent unit at Cottesmore under the control of RAF Support Command, unlike the TTTE the RAF element of which was controlled by HQ 1 Gp STC, the German element by 3 Luftwaffen Division and the Italian element by Rome Air Staff. Others which followed were two nationally funded engineering units: The Tornado Engineering and Development Investigation Team (TEDIT) in July 1980 and the Tornado in Service Software Maintenance Team (TISMT) on 4 August 1980, highlighting the importance of many of the computer based systems in the aircraft.

The first Station Commander was Group Captain M G Simmons AFC, Oberst H Ochsenkuhn represented the GAF and Navy and Colonnello E Raglio (after a short period by Tenente Colonnello G Russo) represented the Italian Air Force. Then as now there were four Wings: Operations, then commanded by Wing Commander Nunn, Engineering, Squadron Leader Highmore followed by Wing

The three elements of TTTE - Italian (closest to camera) German and British Tornadoes in flight. *(Photo: MoD)*

Commander Emery, Administration, Wing Commander Kerrigan, and the Tornado OCU (TOCU). The TOCUs Chief Instructor (CI) is an alternating national appointment: the first was Wing Commander R P O'Brien. There are four flying squadrons. 'A' squadron was commanded initially by a German Navy Officer; Korvetten Kapitan Roesch, 'B' Squadron by Squadron Leader Ball, 'C' Squadron by Tenente Colonnello Pollice ItAF and Standards Squadron by an alternating national representative, the first being Major Jung GAF. The post of Chief Ground Instructor (CGI) also alternates - and the first CGI was Major Flik GAF.

The first two Tornadoes: ZA320 and ZA322 emerged from the grey veils of an overcast sky on 1 July 1980 flown by two BAE crews, Messrs Paul Millet, now Chief Executive in Oman and Olly Heath, and David Eagles, now Deputy Managing Director, Panavia, and Ray Woolett and were welcomed to Cottesmore by Air Vice- Marshal M W P Knight AOC 1 Group. The first aircraft with a TTTE crew: Squadron Leaders Ball and Tebb flew from the airfield on 27 August 1980 and on 2 September the first MBB aircraft arrived from Manching flown by Major Jung and Major von Sivers.

The Station Commander, an RAF Group Captain, is also the UK Senior National Representative at the TTTE. A German and an Italian officer of equivalent rank are the respective Senior National Representatives, and are responsible for all welfare, administrative and disciplinary matters for the German and Italian personnel on base. There are some 1,600 servicemen and 130 civilians permanently employed at the TTTE; the majority are British, since aircraft servicing and support services, although tri-nationally funded, are the responsibility of the UK. All student aircrew are trained to a tri-nationally agreed syllabus and a British student will be taught by an Italian instructor in a German aircraft, or any other tri-national combination, thus increasing the inter-operability between the three Nations' front-line Tornado squadrons and enhancing NATO's overall operational effectiveness.

The first course of TTTE at Cottesmore. L to R (standing) Sqn Ldr Symonds, Flt Lt Smith. (Sitting) KKpt Schumacher, OTL Flik, Gp Capt Simmons, Sqn Ldr Morris. *(Photo MoD)*

TTTE opens for business!
The culmination of the years of preparation was reached on 29 January 1981 when the TTTE was officially opened by the three Chiefs of Air Staff, Air Chief Marshal Sir Michael Beetham, RAF, Generalleutnant Friedrich Obleser, Luftwaffe, and Generale di Squadra Lamberto Bartolucci, Aeronautica Militare Italiana (AMI), and Admiral Günter Fromm, C-in-C Fleet, Kriegsmarine.

It was a spectacular affair which might have been the more so if a formation flypast crewed by aircrew from the three nations planned as part of the ceremony had taken place, but the cloud brushing the tops of the hangars restricted the overflight to a single aircraft crewed by Wing Commander O'Brien and Squadron Leader Morris. It was not seen - but unmistakeably heard.

From its official opening under the TTTE colours with a sprinkling of British, German and Italian aircraft, some trainers, some strike aircraft, numbers gradually built up until the establishment total of 48; 22 German, 19 British and 7 Italian aircraft was complete in August 1982. As numbers increased so did output. The first monthly hours flown in excess of 500 hours came in September 1981; the first with over 1000 sorties in a month in July 1986. Over 60 sorties in a day was first achieved in April 1986 and by March 1991 Main Course Number 154 was passing through its flying phase.

Trying to be good neighbours.
Flying is intensive with first take-offs from 0745 in the morning and last landing as late as midnight in the summertime. In 1986 there were some 85,000 movements from the airfield which is about one third of the yearly total at London/Heathrow, one of the world's busiest airfields; a state of affairs that does not pass unnoticed by the people living in the villages surrounding Cottesmore. With so many movements with an aircraft that tends to announce its presence with a fair amount of gusto, especially in reheat, the TTTE is still faced with the problem that worried the local people when the airfield opened in 1938; noise. As part of the good neighbour policy adopted by all the station commanders at Cottesmore, senior executives and the Community Relations Officer are always ready to talk to the local villagers and their representatives on the council whenever desired and frequent visits are organised to show local people the Station at work.

TTTE crews plan forthcoming sorties *(Photo: MoD)*

An Annual Reception is held to which local dignitaries, officials, farmers and interested parties are invited. It ends with the dusk ceremony of Beating the Retreat. As the Italian, British and German flags are lowered to the sound of the band playing the Sunset Tune, three Tornados make a sudden and spectacular appearance to pull vertically upwards into a majestic finale. It is a coup de theatre which a senior civilian guest said always makes him want to cry. Following a lengthy survey of the noise problem, the Noise Compensation Survey Team reported on 19 June 1987 recommending generous compensation to selected local villages to pay for sound proofing for their houses.

TTTE Flying courses.
The Main Course. The TOCU Main Course is designed for first tourists and consists of four weeks ground school and nine weeks of flying. Although the early students at the TOCU were experienced aircrew, the majority are now first tourists straight from training. The course is an initial conversion to type and prepares the student for the next phase of training at nationally organised Weapon Conversion Units.

Ground School.
The Tornado is a complex aircraft and the aim is to train students to understand not only their own cockpit, but to have a working knowledge of the problems and priorities of the other crew member. During the first two weeks the various aircraft systems are studied. At the same time, synthetic part-task trainers are used, mainly to train the navigators to handle rear seat avionics without the expense of a full simulator sortie. For the last two weeks of the ground school the students complete their systems lecture programme and fly nine simulator sorties as constituted crews. Every effort is made to mix nationalities

Crews from the third Royal Saudi Air Force course at Cottesmore in August 1986.
(Photo: MoD)

and experience levels within these crews. During free time they make use of the extensive self-teaching video library to refresh their systems and procedures knowledge.

The Flying Phase.

The Flying Phase comprises approximately 35 hours flying for student pilots and 28 hours for navigators, with the first crew solo sortie being flown after approximately 8 hours of flying instruction. Subsequent sorties are flown either crew solo or with an Instructor Pilot (IP) or Instructor Navigator (IN), as appropriate. The Main Course flying is split into 8 phases: Transition, Navigation, Formation, Instrument, Simulated Weaponry, Terrain Following, Night and Attack. Initial flying for the student pilot (SP) covers circuit work, instrument flying,

Air Commodore M.G. Simmons hands over command of the station to Grp Capt T.W.G.Carlton on 25 June 1982 *(Photo:MoD)*

general handling and emergency training, while the student navigator (SN) practises low level navigation and fixing techniques, and receives instruction on front seat monitoring. After this the student crews are introduced to close and tactical formation. The Simulated Weapons Phase introduces the SP and SN to low level laydown attacks on simulated targets, practising both visual and IMC techniques. Students also practise Loft attacks, in which the aircraft is flown to a pre-computed Pull-Up Point from which a 3g pull up is made for simulated automatic weapon delivery, followed by an escape manoeuvre to return to low level. Next, the students are introduced to Automatic Terrain Following (ATF), three sorties of which are flown by day in order to give confidence before tackling the three night ATF sorties. During these sorties, simulated targets are included in order to consolidate weaponry techniques and crew co-operation. To round off the course, the students fly as a solo crew on pairs Attack missions to bring all aspects of their training together in a representative tactical situation.

Additional Flying courses.

There are three major additional training courses: Senior Officers Course contains virtually the same amount of ground school and simulator training as the main course, but flying is limited to 12 sorties, providing a brief insight into the various phases of the full course for officers destined for senior command or staff appointments. The Competent to Instruct (C to I) Course is designed to train Instructor Pilots (IPs) and Instructor Navigators (INs) for the TOCU and for operational squadrons. And finally, the Instrument Rating Examiner (IRE) Course which trains experienced Tornado pilots to be IREs. Candidates for the course are already rear seat qualified and already have a Green or Master Green Instrument Rating.

The first hint that the TTTE was soon to temporarily become a four nation establishment was received in August 1985 when a Saudi Arabian delegation visited Cottesmore to make a survey of the facilities available. It was announced during September that Saudi Arabia had signed a letter of intent to buy 48 Tornado strike aircraft and 24 of the air defence version in addition to 30 Hawks and 30 Pilatus PC-9 trainers. Once the decision was made, events at Cottesmore moved with remarkable rapidity. The first Saudi students arrived on 11 October only a few days after the announcement was made that they

Her Majesty the Queen during her visit to TTTE on 13 June 1984. *(Photo: MoD)*

would be trained at Cottesmore. Five Chivenor Hawks arrived on 1 November, on semi permanent attachment for three weeks, and were quickly in action on the Saudi training programme. The following year the first of their Tornados had been delivered to Dhahran in Saudi Arabia. The RAF, ItAF, GAF and Navy squadrons are now up to full strength but training of replacement crews continues unabated although the number of aircraft and staff have been reduced since the period peak in 1986. Saudi Arabian crew training in the UK is complete and they are now operating their 48 Tornados at Dhahran and other bases.

Signor Spadalini, the Italian minister of Defence arrives and is welcomed by Group Captain Terry Carlton at Cottesmore in 1984. *(Photo': MoD)*

Two photographs of the Tornado 'Meet' held at Cottesmore on 14 October 1988.
Below: British, German and Italian aircrew and Instructors pose with representatives from
the Tornadoes manufacturers to celebrate the event. *(Photo's : British Aerospace)*

ACM Sir David Craig, (former CO of 35 Squadron at Cottesmore) after his flight with Sqn Ldr Bernie Mills on 17 October 1986. *(Photo: MoD)*

RAF STC Tornados are based at Marham with 27 and 617 squadrons, and at Honington with 13 Squadron (Recce) and the Tornado Weapons Conversion Unit (TWCU). RAF Germany have IX, 14, 17 and 31 squadrons at Brüggen, and II(AC)(Recce), XV, 16 and 20 squadrons at Laarbruch. Luftwaffe Jagdbombergeschwadern (Wings - Jabog for short), which have two Staffeln (Squadrons) are based at 31 Jabog 'Boelke' at Norvenich, with 311 and 312 staffeln, Jabog 32 at Lechfeld with 321 and 322 staffeln, Jabog 33 at Büchel with 331 and 332 staffeln, Jabog 34 at Memmingen with 341 and 342 staffeln. Jabog 38 is based at Jever with Staffeln 381 (Weapons Conversion Unit), and 382 [Electronic Countermeasures and Reconnaissance (ECR)]. For the Marineflieger, Marinefliegergeschwader 1 (MFG 1) is based on Schleswig and MFG 2 at Eggebeck. The AMI, has 6° Stormo (Wing) at Ghedi with 154 Gruppo (Squadron), 36° Stormo at Gioia del Colle with 156 Gruppo, and 50° Stormo at Piacenza with 155 Gruppo.

Distinguished visitors and flying hazards.
Many famous people have visited Cottesmore during the TTTE years: Caspar Weinberger, American Secretary of Defence in April 1981, Her Majesty Queen Elizabeth II in June 1984, the President of Italy, Signor Francesco Cossiga in November, 1986, the Inspector General of the Luftwaffe, General Altenburg, the Defence Minister of Italy, Signor Spadolini, the Chiefs of Staff of the German and Italian Air Forces, the Hon Valerio Zanone, the Italian Minister of Defence in November 1988, Members of the European and UK Parliaments and of the House of Lords, High Sheriffs, Ambassadors, Air Attachés, distinguished servicemen and civil servants, chairmen of many committees, eminent industrialists and mighty contractors; January 1987 brought Lorenzo de Medici, a worthy diplomat, though not to be confused with Lorenzo the Magnificent. Also in April 1990 the German Ambassador to London arrived with an even more familiar name: Baron von Richtofen. The Ambassador is a great nephew of the dashing First World War pilot Manfred von Richtofen - The Red Baron. Sadly he did not

ACM Sir Neil Wheeler inspects the cockpit of a TTTE Tornado during his visit in 1987. Also in the photograph are Major Fritz Thomsen, Sqn Ldr Forbes Smith and the Station Commander, Group Captain Peter Squire. *(Photo: MoD)*

arrive in a bright red Fokker Triplane, but rather more importantly with a mission 'to deepen Anglo-German friendship and trust'.

It was not long after operations at Cottesmore began that certain hazards to aircraft in the local area became apparent. In the early 1970s Rutland was drained by four gentle trout streams: the Welland, the Chater, the Gwash and the Eye Brook. In 1976 the Vale of Catmose was dammed at Empingham, Rutland Water became a reality and almost immediately the dramatic change in habitat attracted sea birds and waders, marsh loving birds and their predators in spectacular numbers, indeed it is now internationally important for wintering wildfowl many of which have developed a fondness for migrating across the airfield at dawn and dusk. A Tornado's RB199 engine will swallow a swallow with scarcely a burp of protest, however a goose or a swan assumes a more alarming prospect. For this reason certain restrictions are imposed in the circuit at critical times. The En Route Supplement under the Cottesmore heading carries a note in heavy print: CAUTION BIRD HAZARD.

The weather at Cottesmore can also be a hazard - not generally worse than at other RAF airfields in the UK unless the wind swings round to come from the south-east quadrant in moist conditions. If it does, Met Men and Duty Commanders develop haunted looks as the air creeps up the gentle slope from the North Sea rolling the stratus before it to lick its tongue round the corner of the hangars and to rub its back along the window panes of ATC.

Cottesmore's Area Air Traffic Controllers also have a busy time tracking low flying aircraft busily passing in the vicinity of the zone as Wittering, Cranwell, Marham, Honington, Coltishall, Bentwaters, Alconbury and RAF Germany aircraft compete for low level airspace. Partly to lessen the

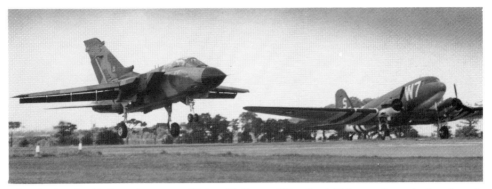

Continuing the Airshow theme - and links with the past Grp Capt. Elder carries out a 'touch and go' alongside the Imperial War Museum's C-47 (43-15509) that wears the markings it carried on 17 September 1944 when it flew on Operation 'Market' *(Photo: N. J. Roberson)*

traffic but primarily to operate in an area of potentially better weather which offers more challenging training, Exercise Winter Venture was first put into effect in November 1986 to maintain the momentum of the summer output. This called for six aircraft to fly for landaway sorties to Machrihanish daily. A ground party travelled by Andover to support the operations, changing over at fortnightly intervals. Since then Winter operations have been carried out at Lossiemouth and Leuchars, the latter being far more accessible by train, or by road if absolutely necessary.

Every year, usually on a Saturday in July, an all ranks, all nations Families Day is held at Cottesmore. This does not always guarantee good weather as the 50th Anniversary Weekend of 10/13 June 1988 demonstrated. On that Saturday, iron grey clouds at 400 feet above the airfield and a forbidding north east wind did their best to spoil the proceedings. This they failed to do as the following extract from the August 1988 edition of Tornado Talk, the Station Magazine made clear:

'As the cloud base slowly lifted during the afternoon, the little aircraft: the Pitts Specials, the Skybolt, the Cranfield A1 Chase, the 5/8 scale Focke Wulf 190 and Spitfire were able to show off their routines below the cloud to some advantage, the fast jets had to limit their shows to the horizontal plain, or thereabouts. It did not seem to make much difference. The Luftwaffe F-104G Starfighter, glowing at one end like a well sucked Havana cigar, scorched the circuit to devastating effect and the Wittering Harriers gave a glimpse of what it must have been like to be on the receiving end of their disapproval at Port Stanley and Goose Green as they demonstrated an airfield attack. The big aircraft were no less impressive: the Tristar, the Catalina, partly owned and flown by Flight Lieutenant John Watts of 'C' Squadron, the Shackleton, which was once described by a crew member as 40,000 loose rivets flying in close formation and the C160 Transall which had a natty end to its display after landing by backing down the runway, turning to salute the crowd and then departing with a short take-off. Such old favourites as the Vulcan lumbered gently in from the west, flown by Squadron Leader McDougall, heaved itself upwards with a groan of monumental indigestion and did a wing over with the port wing in the cloud, the other in the clear, in a nice, if unintended theatrical flourish. Squadron Leader Jerry Pook with Flight Lieutenant Paul Smith, Hauptmann Gerhard Roeder and Major Hans-Helmut Knoke, Maggiore Aldo Gianelli and Capitano Georgio Serravelle in the TTTE Tornado formation flew twice during the afternoon, the first when the cloud base was at its worst and later when it had improved to about 1,000 feet which gave them a little more scope to demonstrate the aircraft effectively. Afterwards six Rolls-Royce Merlins announced the arrival of the Spitfire, Hurricane and Lancaster of the Battle of

Ten Years of Tri-National Tornado Establishment

The personnel, equipment and units of RAF Cottesmore

Britain Memorial Flight. The climax to the day was a display of wondrous smoothness and colour by the Italian National Aerobatic Team, the Frecce Tricolori with their ten Aermacchi MB-339A aircraft. Beside the flying, there was a static aircraft park featuring many NATO aircraft, sideshows and lots of family entertainments. In following years the climax to the show has been provided by the RAF Red Arrows in their Hawks.

The same crews who flew the Cottesmore Tornados on Friday and Saturday flew the flypast over the market square for the 'Freedom of Oakham' ceremony on Sunday. It was a vastly different day, sparkling like Friday night's Official Reception wine and bringing at last the warm breath of summer to the colourful ceremony with the various shades of blue of the uniforms of the three Air Forces and Navy contrasting with the patches of red, yellow, gold and white of the Mayor, Corporation, the Lord Lieutenant of the County and the ladies' hats, all crammed into the pleasant old County Town of Rutland. The parade was led by OC Operations Wing, Wing Commander B Lee, preceded by the Cranwell College Band. On the first 'General Salute' and right on cue, the three Tornados passed overhead.

Many other social and annual functions occur at Cottesmore, including Burns' Night, Italian Night and the Summer Balls in the Officers' and Sergeants' Messes and a combined all ranks Oktoberfest held in one of the hangars which draws devotees from all over the UK and Europe. Dining In and Ladies Guest Nights are held throughout the year where the unique Tri-National spirit of Cottesmore is always conspicuous.

TTTE, which has recently celebrated its 10th Anniversary, is by far the longest serving unit to have been based at RAF Cottesmore and is now under the command of its sixth Commander: Group Captain T W Rimmer OBE MA (formerly the third CI of the TTTE - January 1985 until July 1987) who has succeeded Group Captains M G Simmons AFC, T W G Carlton, P J Goddard AFC, P T Squire DFC AFC and R D Elder. Oberst J Böttcher has followed Obersts H Ochsenkuhn and J Hoppe, and Colonello A Lupo has succeeded Colonellos Raglio and P Ceccarelli. Wing Commander A Dyer-Perry, the fourth OC Ops is in the chair, the fourth Chief Instructor: Colonello T Ferro has recently returned to Italy to be succeeded by Wing Commander R Mclellan; the sixth OC Eng, Wing Commander K Harris and the sixth OC Admin, Wing Commander D Wallace are in post.

In its ten years of operations, the TTTE has had a remarkably good flight safety record. Despite all the variables the TTTE has a significantly lower accident rate than other units engaged on low-flying training sorties. The TTTE suffered the first of two fatal accidents on 17 June 1986 when Leutnant Peter Kastner, a Luftwaffe pilot and his RAF navigator Squadron Leader John Towl were killed when their Tornado struck a hill near the Claerwen Reservoir in Wales in poor weather. Many tributes were paid to the two officers but a remark by Group Captain Sam Goddard in the Cottesmore Station Magazine spoke for all three nations:

'While success has been predominant, the fatal flying accident in June was a sad reminder that the TTTE could suffer setbacks, but in a way, this drew us closer together and spurred us on to new efforts'.

Two years later, on 9 August 1988, Flight Lieutenant John Watts, an RAF pilot and his Luftwaffe navigator, Leutnant Ulrich Sayer, were flying on a low level exercise, part of which passed through the Lake District. Flight Lieutenant Watts' aircraft was heading south in the dusk down the East Fell side of Eden Valley. The crew had just engaged the auto pilot and begun a left turn. When passing through a heading of 139 degrees they were struck on the underside of their aircraft by one of a pair of 617 Squadron Tornados from Marham heading north up the valley. Neither crew saw the other.

The future of TTTE?

Since the first aircraft were delivered in July 1980, the TTTE has trained 154 Main Courses of students by the end of March 1991, totalling more than 2,300 Tornado aircrew. Many of the early graduates have themselves become instructors, either at the TTTE, on weapons conversion units, or on squadrons. The TTTE is committed to the continuation of its task, well into the 1990s. It's achievements so far have demonstrated that three nations can work together professionally and efficiently, while maintaining a friendly and enjoyable atmosphere for everyone involved.

At the end of the TTTE's ten years of operations at Cottesmore, the overall world situation is strikingly improved from its position in 1980 when it arrived, despite deteriorations during 1982 in the Falklands and 1990 when Iraq invaded Kuwait; both salutory reminders that it is unwise to allow ones guard to slip too low. Now, at the end of March 1991, with news of the successful conclusion of hostilities in the Gulf, prospects for lasting peace in the future appear infinitely better than when the airfield was built in the late 1930s.

If, at some time in the dim and misty future, the airfield reverts to fields, woods and hedgerows, ramblers near the village will have cause to tread lightly lest they step upon the bones of wrecked wartime aircraft: Fairey Battles, Handley Page Hampdens and Herefords, Vickers Wellingtons, Avro Lancasters, Junkers Ju 88s and Heinkel 111s, Douglas Skytrains, de Havilland Mosquitos and afterwards de Havilland Tiger Moths, North American Harvards, Percival Prentices, Boulton Paul Balliols, a Handley Page Victor, Avro Vulcans and English Electric Canberras. They may sense the echoes of German, Italian, Arabic, French, Dutch, Canadian, Australian, American and British and other voices, and, with the history of man's fallibility in mind, they may reflect that the TTTE was a bright spot in international co-operation and a hopeful sign for the future.

They may even stumble on that stone left by the Americans in 1945, and read its message: 'May the memory of the comradeship sown in the skies of Europe forever be as green as the fields of Cottesmore'.

SIGNIFICANT DATES & UNITS BASED AT RAF COTTESMORE

Airfield construction commenced		1935
Airfield officially opened		11 Mar 1938
35 Squadron	Wellesley I, Battle I & II, Anson.	20 Apr 1938 - 25 Aug 1939
207 Squadron	Wellesley I, Battle I & II, Anson.	20 Apr 1938 - 24 Aug 1939
185 Squadron	Hampden I, Hereford I, Anson.	24 Aug 1939 - 17 May 1940
106 Squadron	Hampden I, Anson	1 Sep 1939 - 6 Oct 1939
14 OTU	Hampden I, Hereford I, Anson I, Defiant I, Wellington I, IA, IC, II,	8 Apr 1940 - 1 Aug 1943
(Formed from No.185 Sqn)	Lysander III, IIIA, Oxford I and II, Martinet I, Tiger Moth II	
Station under Care and Maintenance		10 Aug 1943 - Mar 1944
2 Heavy Glider MU	Horsa I	26 Aug 1943 - 19 Oct 1943
34 Glider Maintenance Sect	Horsa I	20 Oct 1943 - 17 Feb 1944
Cottesmore became USAAF Station No. 489		28 Sep 1943 - 30 Jun 1945
Three hard surface runways constructed, the longest being 2000 yards.		10 Aug 1943 - Mar 1944
U.S. IXth Air Force 316th TC Group USAAF comprising:		16 Feb 1944 - 14 May 1945
36 TC Sqn	All units operated C-47 Skytrain, C-53 Skytrooper,	
37 TC Sqn	CG-4A (glider), Horsa I, C-46D Commando and C-109	
44 TC Sqn		
45 TC Sqn		
IXth AFTCC Pathfinder School	C-47	28 Feb 1944 - 22 Mar 1945
Station reverted to RAF control		1 Jul 1945
1668 Heavy Conversion Unit	Lancaster I and III, Beaufighter VIF,	15 Sep 1945 - 7 Mar 1946
	Spitfire VB, Mosquito NFXIX	
16 OTU	Mosquito TIII, FBVI and BXVI. Oxford I	22 Mar 1946 - 30 Apr 1947
204 Advanced Flying School	Mosquito TIII and FBVI	1 May 1947 - 1 Mar 1948
(re-named from 16 OTU)		
No.7 FTS	Tiger Moth T2. Harvard IIB, Prentice T1, Balliol T2	1 Mar 1948 - 24 Mar 1954
15 Squadron	Canberra B2	19 Mar 1954 - 15 Feb 1955
44/55 Squadron	Canberra B2	20 May 1954 - 20 Feb 1955
57 Squadron	Canberra B2	22 May 1954 - 15 Feb 1955
149 Squadron	Canberra B2	22 May 1954 - 24 Aug 1954
Station under Care and Maintenance - main runway extended to 3000 yards		15 Feb 1955 - 8 Apr 1958
10 Squadron	Victor B1	15 Apr 1958 - 1 Mar 1964
15 Squadron	Victor B1 and 1A	1 Sep 1958 - 31 Oct 1964
232 OCU, 'C' Flight	Victor B2	1 Nov 1961 - 31 Mar 1963
35 Squadron	Vulcan B2	7 Nov 1964 - 15 Jan 1969
9 Squadron	Vulcan B2	10 Nov 1964 - 26 Feb 1969
12 Squadron	Vulcan B2	17 Nov 1964 - 31 Dec 1967
98 Squadron	Canberra B2, T4 and E15	17 Apr 1969 - 27 Feb 1976
115 Squadron	Varsity T1, Argosy C1 and E1	18 Apr 1969 - 23 Feb 1976
360 Squadron	Canberra T4 and T17	21 Apr 1969 - 5 Aug 1975
231 OCU	Canberra B2 and T4	19 May 1969 - 18 Feb 1976
Trials Flight	Argosy C1	8 Dec 1970 - 22 Jan 1971
Station under Care and Maintenance		31 Mar 1976 - 31 Mar 1978
Tri-national undertaking to establish the TTE signed		8 May 1979 -
First RAF Tornado GR1 arrived		1 Jul 1980 -
First GAF Tornado GR1 arrived		2 Sep 1980 -
TTTE formed		29 Jan 1981 -
First IAF Tornado GR1 arrived		5 May 1982 -

APPENDIX TWO
ROYAL AIR FORCE COTTESMORE & STATION 489
COMMANDING OFFICERS

Wing Commander H V Drew OBE AFC	-	11 Mar 1938 - 30 Apr 1939
Wing Commander E B Grenfell AFC	-	1 May 1939 - 30 Jun 1939
Group Captain E B Grenfell AFC	-	1 Jul 1939 - 6 May 1940
Wing Commander E D Barnes AFC	-	7 May 1940 - 20 May 1940
Group Captain F H Laurence MC	-	21 May 1940 - 2 Sep 1941
Group Captain A P Ritchie AFC	-	10 Sep 1941 - 5 Apr 1942
Group Captain A Leach MC	-	6 Apr 1942 - 7 Jan 1943
Group Captain S Graham MC	-	8 Jan 1943 - 9 Aug 1943
Squadron Leader G D F Keddie	-	10 Aug 1943 - 30 Jun 1945
Lieutenant-Colonel B R Fleet USAAF	-	16 Feb 1944 - 12 May 1944
Lieutenant-Colonel H A Berger USAAF	-	14 May 1944 - 13 Jun 1944
Colonel H A Berger USAAF	-	14 Jun 1944 - 2 Apr 1945
Lieutenant-Colonel W R Washburn USAAF	-	3 Apr 1945 - 14 May 1945
Flight Lieutenant E B Smith	-	1 Jul 1945 - 26 Aug 1945
Flying Officer T C Currie	-	27 Aug 1945 - 6 Sep 1945
Squadron Leader R W Holden	-	7 Sep 1945 - 14 Sep 1945
Group Captain J H T Simpson DSO	-	15 Sep 1945 - 18 Dec 1945
Group Captain H McC White	-	19 Dec 1945 - 21 Mar 1946
Group Captain R A A Cole CBE	-	22 Mar 1946 -12 May 1946
Group Captain N W F Mason	-	13 May 1946 -16 Feb 1947
Group Captain A H S Lucas	-	17 Feb 1947 - 6 Feb 1950
Group Captain D J Alvey OBE	-	7 Feb 1950 - 2 Oct 1952
Group Captain R Sorel-Cameron CBE AFC	-	3 Oct 1952 -28 Mar 1954
Wing Commander G T Wynne-Powell DFC	-	29 Mar 1954 -13 Apr 1954
Group Captain G T B Clayton DFC and Bar	-	14 Apr 1954 -14 Feb 1955
Squadron Leader A Webster DSO DFC	-	15 Feb 1955 - 4 Jul 1957
Wing Commander M H Le Bas DSO AFC	-	15 Jul 1957 - 27 Oct 1957
Group Captain J E Johnson DSO and 2 Bars DFC and Bar	-	28 Oct 1957 17 Dec 1959
Group Captain A D Mitchell DFC and Bar AFC	-	18 Dec 1959 - 7 Feb 1962
Group Captain R H G Weighill DFC	-	8 Feb 1962 -15 Oct 1964
Group Captain E W Wright CBE DFC DFM	-	16 Oct 1964 - 2 Dec 1965
Group Captain J Garden DFC	-	3 Dec 1965 - 1 Jun 1967
Group Captain W J H Roberts	-	2 Jun 1967 -29 May 1969
Group Captain L G A Bastard AFC	-	30 May 1969 - 1 Jul 1971
Group Captain K Kingshott CBE DFC	-	2 Jul 1971 -13 Jul 1973
Group Captain A F Jenkins CVO	-	14 Jul 1973 -26 Jun 1975
Group Captain R B Gubbins	-	27 Jun 1975 -31 Mar 1976
Care and Maintenance	-	Apr 1976 -31 Mar 1978
Wing Commander B N Wanstall	-	1 Apr 1978 -30 Jun 1980
Group Captain M G Simmons AFC	-	1 Jul 1980 -1 Dec 1981
Air Commodore M G Simmons AFC	-	1 Jan 1982 -24 Jun 1982
Group Captain T W G Carlton	-	25 Jun 1982 -29 Nov 1984
Group Captain P J Goddard AFC	-	30 Nov 1984 -27 Nov 1986
Group Captain P T Squire DFC AFC	-	28 Nov 1986 - 9 Nov 1988
Group Captain R D Elder	-	10 Nov 1988 -21 Sep 1990
Group Captain T W Rimmer OBE MA	-	22 Sep 1990 -

APPENDIX THREE
COTTESMORE FLYING UNIT COMMANDERS

Unit	Commander	Dates
35 Squadron	Sqn Ldr A G Thackray	20 Apr 1938 - 4 Sep 1938
	Flt Lt H F Chester	5 Sep 1938 -30 Sep 1938
	Sqn Ldr H F Chester	1 Oct 1938 -25 Aug 1939
207 Squadron	Sqn Ldr J W Lissett	20 Apr 1938 -19 Aug 1938
	Sqn Ldr J N D Anderson	20 Aug 1938 -31 Mar 1938
	Wg Cdr J N D Anderson	1 Apr 1939 -24 Aug 1939
185 Squadron	Wg Cdr E D Barnes AFC	24 Aug 1939 -17 May 1940
106 Squadron	Sqn Ldr W C Sheen	1 Sep 1939 - 6 Oct 1939
14 OTU	Gp Capt E B Grenfell AFC	8 Apr 1940 - 6 May 1940
	Wg Cdr E D Barnes AFC	7 May 1940 -20 May 1940
	Gp Capt F H Laurence MC	21 May 1940 - 2 Sep 1941
	Wg Cdr D D Christie	3 Sep 1941 - 9 Sep 1941
	Gp Capt A P Ritchie AFC	10 Sep 1941 - 5 Apr 1942
	Gp Capt A Leach MC	6 Apr 1942 - 7 Jan 1943
	Gp Capt S Graham MC	8 Jan 1943 - 1 Aug 1943
36 TCS	Maj J R Farris USAAF	16 Feb 1944 -12 May 1944
	Maj J L Roberts USAAF	12 May 1944 -22 Jun 1944
	Maj G Wright USAAF	23 Jun 1944 - 6 Feb 1945
	Lt Col G Wright USAAF	7 Feb 1945 -14 May 1945
37 TCS	Maj L C Fletcher USAAF	16 Feb 1944 -17 Oct 1944
	Lt Col L C Fletcher USAAF	18 Oct 1944 -14 May 1945
44 TCS	Maj B F Kendig USAAF	16 Feb 1944 -17 Oct 1944
	Lt Col B F Kendig USAAF	18 Oct 1944 -14 May 1945
45 TCS	Maj M Lewis USAAF	16 Feb 1944 -18 Oct 1944
	Lt Col M Lewis USAAF	19 Oct 1944 -24 Mar 1945
	Maj J L Hoggat USAAF	25 Mar 1945 -14 May 1945
IXth AFTCC Pathfinder School	Lt Col J L Crouch USAAF	28 Feb 1944 -22 Mar 1944
1668 HCU	Gp Capt J H T Simpson DSO	15 Sep 1945 -18 Dec 1945
	Gp Capt H McC White	19 Dec 1945 - 7 Mar 1946
16 OTU	Gp Capt R A A Cole CBE	22 Mar 1946 -12 May 1946
	Gp Capt N W F Mason	13 May 1946 -16 Feb 1947
	Gp Capt A H S Lucas	17 Feb 1947 -30 Apr 1947
204 AFS	Gp Capt A H S Lucas	1 May 1947 - 1 Mar 1948
7 FTS	Gp Capt A H S Lucas	16 Mar 1948 - 6 Feb 1950
	Gp Capt D J Alvey OBE	7 Feb 1950 - 2 Oct 1952
	Gp Capt R Sorel-Cameron CBE AFC	3 Oct 1952 -24 Mar 1954
15 Squadron	Sqn Ldr J M Ayshford DFC	19 May 1954 -15 Feb 1955
44/55 Squadron	Sqn Ldr S E Balfour AFC	20 May 1954 -20 Feb 1955
57 Squadron	Sqn Ldr I G Broom DSO DFC AFC	22 May 1954 - 2 Nov 1954
	Sqn Ldr J F Rothwell	3 Nov 1954 -15 Feb 1955
149 Squadron	Sqn Ldr R E R Adams	22 May 1954 -24 Aug 1954
10 Squadron	Wg Cdr C B Owen DSO DFC AFC	15 Apr 1958 -14 Feb 1960
	Wg Cdr R B Phillips DFC AFC	15 Feb 1960 -28 Jan 1962
	Wg Cdr T C Gledhill AFC	29 Jan 1962 - 1 Mar 1964
15 Squadron	Wg Cdr D A Green DSO OBE DFC	1 Sep 1958 -31 Dec 1959
	Gp Capt D A Green DSO OBE DFC	1 Jan 1960 -31 Mar 1960
	Wg Cdr J G Matthews AFC	1 Apr 1960 -30 Nov 1962
	Wg Cdr N G S Marshall	1 Dec 1962 -31 Oct 1964
232 OCU, C Flt	Sqn Ldr G H Burleigh AFC	1 Nov 1961 -31 Mar 1963
35 Squadron	Wg Cdr D B Craig	7 Nov 1964 -31 May 1965
	Wg Cdr D A Arnott DFC	1 Jun 1965 -18 Jun 1967
	Wg Cdr H S Carver MVO	19 Jun 1967 -15 Jan 1969
9 Squadron	Wg Cdr J E Pollington	10 Nov 1964 -19 Dec 1966
	Wg Cdr A M Christie	20 Dec 1966 -26 Jun 1968
	Wg Cdr J E Sewell MBE	27 Jun 1968 -26 Feb 1969
12 Squadron	Wg Cdr J R Tanner	17 Nov 1964 -24 May 1966
	Wg Cdr D H Tew AFC	25 May 1966 -31 Dec 1967
98 Squadron	Sqn Ldr J N Landeryou	17 Apr 1969 - 8 Jul 1970
	Sqn Ldr R Feakes	9 Jul 1970 -12 Mar 1972
	Sqn Ldr R R Taylor MBE	13 Mar 1972 -22 Jun 1972
	Sqn Ldr M R Killick	23 Jun 1972 -23 Jun 1974

	Sqn Ldr M H Wilson	24 Jun 1974 -27 Feb 1976
115 Squadron	Wg Cdr H B C Broadmeadow	18 Apr 1969 - 7 Dec 1970
	Wg Cdr R G Ashford MBE	8 Dec 1970 -10 Dec 1972
	Wg Cdr M J W Lee	11 Dec 1972 - 2 Jan 1975
	Wg Cdr R F Grattan	3 Jan 1975 -23 Feb 1976
360 Squadron	Wg Cdr R M Dubock AFC	21 Apr 1969 -19 Mar 1970
	Wg Cdr L W F Wheeler	20 Mar 1970 -28 Sep 1972
	Cdr G Oxley RN	29 Sep 1972 -17 Oct 1974
	Wg Cdr D R Watson MBE	18 Oct 1974 - 5 Aug 1975
231 OCU	Sqn Ldr T H Stonor BSc	19 May 1969 -25 Nov 1969
	Sqn Ldr R R Taylor MBE	26 Nov 1969 - 7 Mar 1972
	Sqn Ldr D A P Merriman MA	8 Mar 1972 -12 Sep 1974
	Sqn Ldr M J Purdie	13 Sep 1974 -18 Feb 1976
TTTE	Gp Capt M G Simmons AFC	1 Jul 1980 -31 Dec 1981
	Air Cdre M G Simmons AFC	1 Jan 1982 -24 Jun 1982
	Gp Capt T W G Carlton	25 Jun 1982 -29 Nov 1984
	Gp Capt P J Goddard AFC	30 Nov 1984 -27 Nov 1986
	Gp Capt P T Squire DFC AFC	28 Nov 1986 - 9 Nov 1988
	Gp Capt R D Elder	10 Nov 1988 -21 Sep 1990
	Gp Capt T W Rimmer OBE MA	22 Sep 1990 -

TTTE
CHIEF INSTRUCTORS AND SQUADRON COMMANDERS

Chief Instructor	Wg Cdr R P O'Brien	RAF	Jul 1980 - Feb 1983
	OTL K Kahlert	GAF	Feb 1983 - Jan 85
	Wg Cdr T W Rimmer	RAF	Jan 1985 - Jul 1987
	T Col T Ferro	ITAF	Jul 1987 - Jan 1989
	Col T Ferro	ITAF	Jan 1989 - Jan 1990
	Wg Cdr R McLellan	RAF	Jan 1990 -
OC Standards Squadron	Maj H Jung	GAF	Aug 1980 - Mar 1983
	Sqn Ldr M R W Crook	RAF	Mar 1983 - Aug 1985
	T Col G Papele	ITAF	Aug 1985 - Nov 1987
	Sqn Ldr D Hammond	RAF	Nov 1987 - Sep 1989
	Maj R Offinger	GAF	Sep 1989 -
OC 'A' Squadron	K Kpt J Roesch	GNY	Jan 1981 - Sep 1984
	Maj D Kestermann	GAF	Sep 1984 - Jul 1988
	K Kpt R Seeland	GNY	Jul 1988 -
OC 'B' Squadron	Sqn Ldr M W Ball	RAF	Aug 1980 - Aug 1983
	Sqn Ldr B J Mills	RAF	Aug 1983 - Nov 1986
	Sqn Ldr P Chandler	RAF	Nov 1986 - Oct 1988
	Sqn Ldr W J Ramsey	RAF	Oct 1988 -
OC 'C' Squadron	T Col E Pollice	ITAF	Jun 1981 - Jun 1982
	T Col F Cariati	ITAF	Jun 1982 - Jul 1983
	T Col M Redditi	ITAF	Jul 1983 - Aug 1984
	T Col G Bergamini	ITAF	Aug 1984 - Aug 1985
	T Col A Tassarotti	ITAF	Aug 1985 - Jan 1986
	T Col P Viola	ITAF	Jan 1986 - Aug 1988
	T Col A Gianelli	ITAF	Aug 1988 - Aug 1990
	T Col B D'Agata	ITAF	Aug 1990 -
Chief Ground Instructor	OTL J Flik	GAF	Aug 1980 - Jul 1983
	Sqn Ldr G Gardner	RAF	Jul 1983 - Jul 1985
	Maj R M Schuegraf	GAF	Jul 1985 - Sep 1987
	Sqn Ldr K C Eaton	RAF	Spe 1987 - Jun 1989
	Maj G J Prill	GAF	Jun 1989 -

COTTESMORE AIRCRAFT AND CODES

35 Sqn — Code letters: **WT**

Anson I

| N5264 | N5265 |

Wellesley I

| K7739 | K7747 | K7749 | K7750 | K7752 | K7754 | K7755 | K7768 |
| K7770 | K8526 | K8529 | K8530 (35-G) | L2642 | L2688 | | |

Battle I

K7588	K7590	K7592	K7593	K7595	K7596	K7597	K7598
K7600	K7619	K7620	K7624	K7629	K7673	K7675	K7677
K7678	K7680	K7693	K7694	K7695	K7705	K7706	K7707
K7708 (N)	K7709	K7710	K7711	K7712 (C)	K9176	K9177	K9178
K9179	K9180	K9182 (J)	K9183	K9246	K9330	K9457	K9466
K9469	K9470	K9471 (WT-M)		K9472	K9473	K9474	K9475
K9476	K9478	K9479	K9480	K9481	L4974	L4975	L4976
L4977	L4978	L4980	L4981	L5183	L5197	L5202	L5203
L5263	L5264	L5265	L5266	L5267	L5268	L5269	L5270
L5271	L5272	L5273					

207 Sqn — Code letters: **NJ**

Anson I

| N5266 | N5267 |

Wellesley I

| K7756 | K7757 | K7758 | K7759 | K7760 | K7761 | K7762 | K7763 |
| K7764 | K7765 | K7769 | K8531 | K8532 | | | |

Battle I

K7571	K7573	K7576	K7578	K7580	K7581	K7582	K7583
K7584	K7585	K7601	K7628	K7674	K7684	K7685	K7690
K9181	K9185	K9186	K9187	K9188	K9189	K9190	K9191
K9192	K9193	K9194 (T)	K9195	K9196 (A)	K9197	K9198	K9200 (Z)
K9336	K9448	K9450	K9451	K9452	K9453	K9454	K9455
K9458	K9459	K9460	K9461	K9462	K9463	K9464	K9465 (N)
L4962 (NJ-)	L4963	L4964	L4965	L4966	K4967	L5185	L5228
L5274	L5275	L5276	L5277	L5278	L5279	L5280	L5281
L5282	L5283	L5284	L5482				

185 Sqn — Code letters: **ZM, GL**

Anson I

| N5085 | N5093 | N5110 | N5208 | N5211 | N5212 | N9830 | N9831 |
| N9832 (GL-L) | N9833 | N9834 | R3399 | | | | |

Hampden I

L4191	L4192	L9193	L4194 (ZM-B)	L4195	L4196	L4197	L4198
L4199	L4200	L4201	L4203	L4204	L4205	L4206	P1274
P1275	P1276	P1279					

Hereford I

| L6005 | L6007 | L6008 | L6011 | L6012 | L6016 |

106 Sqn — Code letters: **XS, ZN**

Anson I

| N5262 (L) | N5163 | N5164 | N5166 (XS-X) |

Hampden I

L4149							L4180
L4174 (ZN-A)	L4175 (ZN-B)	L4176	L4177	L4178			
L4181 (ZN-J)	L4182 (ZN-O)	L4183 (ZN-P)	L4184 (ZN-Q)	L4185 (ZN-S)	L4186 (ZN-T)
L4187 (ZN-U)	L4188 (ZN-V)	L4189			

14 OTU — Code letters: **AM, GL, VB**

Anson I

K6186	K8824	L7924	N4911	N4989 (G)	N5037	N5064 (W1)
N5079	N5093	N5110	N5166 (Z1 & C)	N5169	N5211	N5259
N5323	N5325	N9605	N9608	N9829	N9830	N9831
N9832	N9833	N9834	N9848	N9903	N9905	N9912 (D2)
N9991	R3310	R3386 (W1)	R3398	R3399	R3445 (Q2)	R3587 (Y)
R9602 (J2)	R9603	R9604 (K)	R9605	R9606 (N3 & N2)	R9607 (VB-02)	R9608 (VB-Z)
R9609	R9644	R9645	R9646 (F1)	R9647 (L)	R9690	R9692
R9718	R9748	R9749	R9750	R9752	R9753	R9754
W1879	AW974 (A)	AW978 (G2)	AW982 (R2)	AX107 (N2)	AX108	

Hampden I

L4038	L4041	L4048	L4070 (M3)	L4075	L4076	L4086
L4100 (N1)	L4105(G3,B&Ā)	L4108	L4109 (O1 & S)	L4110 (N1)	L4117 (N)	
L4131(K,K1&Ā)	l4133 (F)	L4162 (X & O)	L4173 (T2)	L4193 (M)	L4196 (T1)	L4197
L4198	L4200	L4201 (GL-T)	L4204 (J2&GL-H)	L6020	L6055	L6063 (GL-P)
L6096	N9062 (W3)	P1151 (S2)	P1155	P1157 (Y)	P1158	P1167 (Y3)
P1168	P1176	P1185 (B2)	P1186	P1188 (F1)	P1195 (X2)	P1196
P1204 (A & A1)	P1205 (D1)	P1209 (AM-H3)	P1211	P1213	P1215	P1216 (L3&H)
P1217 (H)	P1230 (Z3)	P1235 (U1)	P1238 (H1)	P1240	P1241	P1242
P1243 (P3)	P1249	P1254	P1265 (T3)	P1272	P1273	P1274
P1275 (GL-M)	P1276 (AM-M1)	P1277	P1278	P1280	P1281	P1282
P1283	P1286 (D)	P1289	P1291 (G & G1)	P1292	P1293 (A2 & M)	P1294
P1298	P1300	P1301	P1303	P1305	P1309	P1310
P1312	P1316 (GL-P)	P1322 (D3)	P1335	P1342 (N1)	P1343	P1344
P1345 (B)	P1346	P1251	P1352	P1353 (C3 & J)	P2062	P2064
P2067 (P2 & P1)	P2072	P2074	P2075	P2076	P2088	P2092
P2112	P2116 (L2)	P2118	P2119	P2120	P2127	P2128
P2129 (P3)	P2138 (P)	P2139 (M1)	P4300	P4303	P4306	P4307
P4308	P4309	P4311	P4312	P4313	P4314	P4315
P4316	P4137	P4318 (O)	P4391	P4395	P4397	P4418 (Q)
P5311 (A3 & V)	P5312 (J3)	P5320($\overline{C}$)	P5321 (P3)	P5322 (U3)	P5344 (Y1)	P5387
P5397 (V3)	P5398	X2972 (P & $\overline{F}$)	X2974	X2980 (Q1)	X2989	X2992
X3061 (O)	X3116	X3142 (L2 & L)	AD736 (W & D)	AD740 (E&R3)	AD741 (B)	AD749
AD751	AD757 (O)	AD758	AD766 (S1)	AD782	AD786	
AD787(C1&M1)	AD792	AD798 (U & X)	AD802 (V1)	AD838(W)	AD845 (V & $\overline{B}$)	AD848 (G)
AD851 (G)	AD860 (D3)	AD906	AD938 (O3 & T)	AD985(K3&N)	AD988	AE155 (S&S2)
AE186	AE190	AE192 (J & C)	AE295	AE312(Q1&S3)	AE386	AE442 (L3)
AT.195	AT2.22($\overline{P}$)	AT223 (P)				

Hereford I

L6008	L6011	L6012	L6014	L6016	L6020	L6025
L6035	L6036	L6037	L6047	L6048	L6052	L6055
L6061	L6062	L6063	L6065	L6070 (GL-A2)	L6073	L6074
L6075	L6088	L6096				

Wellington I

L4219   L4350   L4380

Wellington Ia

N2981

Wellington Ic

L7580 (VB-Y)	L7855	L7869	L7895 (Z)	L7897	L7898	N2772
N2819 (P & X)	N2858 (S & Q)	R1019	R1039 (J)	L1048	R1077	R1140 (Y)
R1224	R1236 (M & D)	R1240 (H)	R1274 (R)	R1295 (P)	R1338	R1398
R1401	R1436	R1522 (Q)	R1592	R1603	R1621	R1669
R1709 (Q)	R1720	R1796 (B)	R1797 (S & T)	R3206 (J & T)	T2511	T2558
T2738	T2887	T2901 (Q)	T2914	T2920	W5629	W5667
W5669	X3163	X3165	X9605	X9608	X9680	X9791
X9796 (H & K)	X9871 (V & N)	X9927	X9944	X9945	X9949	X9953
Z1068	Z1075 (F)	Z1092	Z1095	Z1140 (Y)	Z1154	Z1169 (Y)
Z1171	Z8767	Z8837	Z8856 (P)	Z8896	Z8943	Z8949
Z8963 (Z&AM-G)	Z8970 (Z)	Z8977	Z8982 (R)	AD594(O&GL-U)	AD600 (B)	
AD628 (AM-M)	DV435	DV443	DV449	DV479 (A)	DV486	DV494
DV565 (Q,R & T)	DV666 (Z)	DV668	DV678	DV696	DV697 (J)	DV719
DV730(F)	DV780	DV822	DV823	DV839	DV842	DV864
DV891 (N)	DV897 (P)	DV898 (Q)	DV917	DV921(AM-O)	DV929	HD943 (K)
HD945	HD983 (W)	HD990 (H)				

Wellington II

W5352

Defiant

N1767

Lysander III

R9013   T1504   T1553

Lysander IIIa

V9845

Martinet TT1

HP522 (AM-B)   HP523   HP524   JN596

Oxford I

V3876 (W)	V3993	V3994 (R)	V3996	V4020	V4021	V4199 (U)
V4201	V4203 (S)	AT479	AT480	AT481	AT485	

Oxford II

AS902   AS903 (K2)   AS904   BM833   BM834   BM835

Tiger Moth II

T5983

Horsa I

DP379	DP603	DP622	DP627	DP663	DP670	DP707
HG736	HG745	HG770	HG798	HG801	HG803	HG835
HG840	HG844	HG846	HG917	HS121	HS125	LG699

LG763	LG765	LG838	LH950	LH962	LJ208	LJ229
LJ230	LJ231	LJ232	LJ233	LJ234		

316th TCG
C-47 Skytrain

42-23503	42-23931	42-24387	42-92056	42-92729	42-92884	42-93753
42-93754	42-93755	42-93780	42-100517	42-100546	42-100973	42-108902
42-108909	43-15151 (O)	43-15185	43-15205	43-15227	43-15258	43-15265
43-15300	43-15614 (V)	43-15638	43-15643	43-30652	43-47972	

C-53 Skytrooper
42-68765	42-68766

C-109
42-51982	42-52033 (M)

CG-4A

42-04881	42-07917	42-42025	42-42678	42-47427	42-56187	42-56194
42-56206	42-56219	42-56226	42-56232	42-56253	42-56254	42-56266
42-56275	42-56279	42-56289	42-56324	42-56488	42-56490	42-56499
42-56507	42-56510	42-56548	42-56556	42-56826	42-62133	42-62733
42-73565	42-73568	42-73838	42-73844	42-73880	42-73884	42-73885
42-73917	42-73952	42-74014	42-74024	42-74029	42-74044	42-74063
42-75880	42-77330	42-77345	42-77355	42-77385	42-77393	42-77447
42-77480	42-77500	42-77538	42-77587	42-77624	42-77627	42-77634
42-77654	42-77663	42-77665	42-77674	42-77695	42-77710	42-77895
42-79081	42-79125	42-79132	42-79133	42-79134	42-79137	42-79142
42-79148	42-79254	42-79451	42-79457	42-79465	43-13868	43-15254
43-19725	43-19727	43-19735	43-19751	43-19791	43-19807	43-19824
43-19843	43-19914	43-19915	43-19948	43-26919	43-27348	43-27361
43-27416	43-27441	43-27632	43-36642	43-36654	43-36756	43-36916
43-36935	43-36944	43-36966	43-37287	43-32797	43-37300	43-37322
43-37328	43-37337	43-37382	43-37390	43-37391	43-37399	43-37403
43-37410	43-38804	43-38805	43-39670	43-39678	43-39707	43-39727
43-39781	43-39790	43-39802	43-39804	43-39805	43-39807	43-39808
43-39811	43-39815	43-39844	43-39892	43-39905	43-39944	43-39994
43-40042	43-40051	43-40055	43-40118	43-40119	43-40160	43-40214
43-40244	43-40357	43-40382	43-40386	43-40388	43-40399	43-40421
43-40 424	43-40449	43-40451	43-40521	43-40532	43-40535	43-40544
43-40549	43-40551	43-40552	43-40554	43-40569	43-40576	43-40579
43-40583	43-40795	43-40934	43-41035	43-41095	43-41099	43-41101
43-41141	43-41153	43-41163	43-41165	43-41172	43-41180	43-41183
43-41206	43-41207	43-41210	43-41409	43-41439	43-41506	43-41577
43-41582	43-41610	43-41675	43-41689	43-41699	43-41701	43-41865
43-41889	43-41897	43-41898	43-41921	43-41960	43-41963	43-42021
43-42025	43-42030	43-42035	43-42037	43-42044	43-42045	43-42048
43-42 049	43-42055	43-42089	43-42114	43-42117	43-42118	43-42139
43-42159	43-43057	43-56275	43-59190	43-73587	43-77643	43-79114
43-79142	43-79148	43-79457	43-87300	43-195851	43-197510	43-405351
43-596657	43-840214					

Horsa I

DP379	DP603	DP622	DP627	DP663	DP670	DP707
HG745	HG770	HG798	HG801	HG803	HG840	HG844
HG846	HG917	HS121	HS125	LG699	LG763	LG765
LG838	LH950	LH962	LJ208	LJ227	LJ229	LJ230
LJ231	LJ232	LJ233	LJ234			

36 TC Sqn   Code Letters: 4C

C-46D
44-77613 (Y)

C-47
42-23935	43-15179 (H)	43-15634 (V)	43-30721

C-53
42-68769 (A)

37 TC Sqn   Code Letters: W7

C-47

42-24328	42-24392	42-92725	42-92846	42-93734	42-100502	42-100875
43-15093 (K)	43-15171	43-15212	43-15292 (B)	43-15295	43-15498	43-15509 (S)
15510	43-15617(V)	43-16263	43-16265	43-16266	43-16269	43-16270
43-16273	43-16281	43-30731	43-48263	43-48293	43-48394	43-48399
43-48402	43-48403	43-48414	43-48415	43-48721	43-48722	43-48948
43-48949	43-49682	43-49685	43-93100			

44 TC Sqn — Code Letters: 6E
C-47

42-23505	42-24189	42-24269 (C)	42-92777	42-92886	42-93815	42-100516
43-15095	43-15317 (R)	43-15324 (D)	43-15513	43-15671 (W)	43-48293 (X)	43-48390

C-53

42-68772 (A)

45 TC Sqn — Code Letters: T3
C-47

42-23639	42-24181	42-92832	42-92861	42-93075	42-93511	42-93512
42-100499	42-100883	43-15106	43-15184	43-15194	43-15207	43-15225
43-15305	43-15334	43-15495 (J)	43-15497	43-15633	43-15641	43-15648
43-15659	43-16122					

1668 HCU — Code Letters: J9, 2K
Beaufighter VIf

V8615 (2K-T)	MM854	ND234

Lancaster I

L7580	R5507 (J9-Y)	HK705 (J9-S)	HK732	LL795	LM170 (2K-D&X) LM188
LM287	NF968	NG142	NG274	NG295 (2K-N)	NG383 (2K-G) NN807
NN811	NN812	PD424 (B)	SW252		

Lancaster III

JB551	LM368	LM438	LM717	LM744	ME315 (2K-L) ME329/G (U)
ME569 (D)	ND348(2K-C)	ND747	ND749/G (2K-H)	ND875	ND877 ND909 (J9-L)
ND918	ND965	ND980 (J9-N)	NE120	PB375	PB381 PB437
PB487	PB489	PB506	PB508	PB577	PB584 PB611
PB627	PB681	PB867			

Mosquito XIX

TA342	TA357

Spitfire Vb

W3656	BL328

16 OTU — Code Letters: GA, JS
Mosquito T.III

HJ853	HJ870	HJ898	HJ985	LR567	RR288 RR289(GA-L)
RR292(GA-F)	RR293	TV976	TW108	VA874	

Mosquito FB VI

SZ973 (GA-S)

Mosquito D.XVI

ML938	ML974	ML983	PF481	PF482 (JS-B)	PF483 PF484
PF488 (GA-T)	PF492	PF498	PF510	PF512 JS-E)	PF513 PF538
PF540	PF595	PF597	PF601	PF602	PF609 RV307
RV317	RV347	RV360	RV361	RV363	VA874

Oxford I

LX359	PG988	PH468	PH469	PH471	PH474 PH483
PH484	PH485	PH522			

204 AFS — Code Letters: FMO
Mosquito T.III

HJ898 (E)	HJ985 (D)	LR567 (D)	LR581 (J)	RR288 (C)	RR292 (F) RR316 (A)
TV959 (B)	TV976 (H)	TV981	TW112 (G)	VA871 (G)	VT606 (L)

Mosquito FB.VI

HR175 (Y)	HR242 (Y)	HR252 (X)	HR494	PZ303	RF936 (V) RS551 (O)
RS624 (N)	RS643	RS644	RS698 (M)	SZ973 (S)	SZ975 (Z) TA381
TA476	TA546 (T)	TE590			

Station Flight
Oxford I

LX359

7 FTS — Code Letters: FBA to FBE until 1951 then O, N/M, P/ D,Q
Tiger Moth

N9278	N9506 (FBC-E)	R4833 (FBC-L)	R4941 (FBC-M)	R4956 R5083
R5133	R5136	R5139 (FBC-A)	R5206	T5427 (FBC-Y) T5465 (FBC-W)
T5672 (FBC-Z)		T5700 (FBC-P)	T5842	T6043 (FBC-T) T6497
T6531	T6562 (FBC-B)	T7040 (FBC-Q)	T7129 (FBC-F)	T7332 T7412 (FBC-G)
T7810	T7867	T7870	DE153	DE172 (FBC-C) DE450
DE455	DE482	DE588	DE606	DE615 (FBC-K) DE634
DE658 (FBC-U)	DE853	DE854 (FBC-B)	DE877(FBC-O)	EM814 EM904
EM905 (FBC-N)	NL993	NM115 (FBC-R)		

Harvard IIb

FE908	FE948 (O-Q)	FS738 (O-K)	FS757	FS758 FS776(FBA-L)

FS816   FS822   FS849(FBC-L)   FS850   FS894 (O-W)   FT153 (FBB-F)
FT254 (N-L)   FT255   FT258 (N-H)   FT303 (N-V)   FT319 (O-M)   FT321
FT346   FT376   FT393 (FBB-K)   FT394 (P-B & N-B)   FT412 (FBA-J)   FT413
FT418 (FBB-A&N-G)   FT431(FBA-X&N-K)   FT435 (O-L)   FT436   FT440 (FBB-W)
FX220 (N-A)   FX226 (FBA-K)   FX240(FBB-L&O-V)   FX263 (N-S)   FX266   FX284
FX300 (FBC-U)   FX324 (FBA-M)   FX334 (O-G)   FX376   FX388 (O-O)   FX397 (FBB-B)
FX400   FX428   FX469 (FBA-A)   KF142 (N-J)   KF153 (FBA-H&P-A)   KF156
KF185 (FBA-Q)   KF206 (FBD-N)   KF224 (FBA-V)   KF233   KF238 (FBA-S&P-A)   KF243 (N-D)
KF265 (FBA-P)   KF266(FBA-G&N-G)   KF276   KF288 (O-E & N-F)   KF289 (FBA-U)   KF290 (O-U)
KF300 (FBA-F)   KF333 (N-O)   KF356   KF362   KF364 (FBA-F&N-C)   KF388
KF396   KF472 (FBB-L&O-T)   KF481(FBA-D&N-Q)   KF496 (FBA-T)   KF565 (O-Y)
KF588 (FBB-G&N-R)   KF590 (FBA-E&N-E)   KF605 (FBA-O)   KF633 (FBA-R)   KF661
KF665 (N-U)   KF668   KF688 (FBA-C)   KF691   KF695   KF698 (FBA-L)
KF714 (N-T)   KF725   KF753   KF922 (FBB-Z)   KF924 (N-K)   KF955 (FBB-R)
KF959 (FBA-W)

Balliol T.2

VR593   VR594   VR595 (Q-C)   VR598 (Q-C)   WF989 (D-E & Q-Q)   WF990
WF991   WF992 (Q-D)   WF993 (Q-C)   WF995   WF996   WF997 (Q-E)
WF998   WG110   WG111   WG112 (Q-A)   WG113 (Q-J)   WG114 (Q-U)
WG115 (Q-V)   WG116 (Q-W)   WG117   WG118   WG119 (D-O)   WG120 (D-Q)
WG121 (D-R)   WG122 (Q-J)   WG123 (D-S)   WG124 (D-T)   WG126 (D-U)   WG127 (D-V)
WG128 (D-W)   WG129   WG130 (D-C)   WG131 (D-A)   WG132 (D-B)   WG133 (D-C)
WG134 (D-D)   WG135 (D-E)   WG136 (D-F)   WG137   WG138 (D-G)   WG139 (D-H)
WG140   WG141   WG179   WG186   WG209 (D-K)   WN507 (Q-J)

Prentice T.1

VR219 (FBD-N & M-T)   VR220 (FBD-V & M-Y)   VR221 (P-Z)
VR222 (FBD-)   VR223 (FBE-D,M-W &P-Z)   VR224 (FBD-A & M-M)
VR225 (FBE-H)   VR231 (FBD-F, FBD-H, FBE-J, M-J & M-P)   VR234 (FBD-B & FBE-Z)
VR268 (FBD-S & M-U)   VR278 (FBD-K)   VR285 (FBE-K & M-K)
VR291 (FBD-B,FBE-A,FBE-F & M-X)   VR294   VR303 (P-X)
VR309 (FBE-J)   VR310 (FBE-R & M-N)   VR311 (FBD-F & M-O)
VR312 (FBD-G & M-A)   VR317 (FBD-R & M-E)   VR318 (FBE-G)
VR319 (P-E)   VR320 (FBD-Z)   VR321 (FBE-F & M-J)
VR322 (FBD-Y,M-A,M-G,M-Q)   VR323 (FBE-E)   VR247 (FBD-O & M-D)
VS272   VS290 (FBE-C)   VS318 (P-Y)
VS322 (FBD-Q)   VS325   VS327 (M-Z)
VS354 (FBD-J & M-H)   VS357 (FBD-L & M-C)   VS359 (FBD-T &M-L)
VS365 (FBD-M, M-J & M-S)   VS376 (FBD-X & M-H)   VS383(FBD-U,FBD-Y,M-F&M-J)
VS410 (M-O & M-Q)   VS609 (FBE-J,P-C & P-E)   VS648 (M-B & M-P)
VS649 (M-R)

15 Sqn
Canberra B2

| WH724 | WH725 | WH731 | WH907 | WJ575 | WJ647 | WJ717 | WJ724 | WJ972 | WJ974 |
| WJ976 | WJ985 | | | | | | | | |

44 Sqn
Canberra B2

| WH707 | WH714 | WH717 | WH718 | WH719 | WH856 | WH857 | WH858 | WH908 | WH920 |
| WJ566 | WJ607 | WJ981 | | | | | | | |

57 Sqn
Canberra B2

| WD996 | WH712 | WH720 | WH859 | WH860 | WH878 | WJ568 | WJ574 | WJ575 | WJ621 |
| WJ645 | WJ974 | WJ977 | WK131 | | | | | | |

149 Sqn
Canberra B2

| WD957 | WH711 | WH713 | WH855 | WJ564 | WJ567 | WJ569 | WJ570 | WJ612 | WJ626 |
| WJ973 | | | | | | | | | |

Station Flight
Canberra T4   WH850   WJ863
Anson C19   VL335

Chipmunk T10   WG463

10 Sqn
Victor B1

XA921	XA924	XA927	XA928	XA929	XA930	XA931	XA932	XA935	XA936
XA937	XA938	XA939	XA940	XA941					

15 Sqn
Victor B1

XA935	XA938	XA939	XA940	XA941	XH588	XH589	XH590	XH592	XH593
XH594									

Victor B1A

XA925	XH587	XH591	XH613	XH615	XH616	XH618	XH620	XH648	XH651

232 OCU 'C' Flight
Victor B2   XL165   XL188   XL189   XL230

Station Flight
Anson C19 TX196   VV306
Chipmunk T10   WB645   WG464   WG483   WP783   WP831   WP851

Cottesmore Wing (9, 12 & 35 Squadrons)
Vulcan B2

XH557	XH560	XH561	XH562	XJ780	XJ782	XJ783	XJ823	XJ824	XJ825
XL391	XL445	XM569	XM570	XM571	XM572	XM597	XM598	XM599	XM600
XM602	XM603	XM604	XM605	XM606	XM607	XM608	XM609	XM610	XM611
XM612	XM645	XM646	XM647	XM648	XM649	XM650	XM651	XM652	XM653
XM654	XM655	XM656	XM657						

Station Flight
Chipmunk T10   WD328   WG318   WK633

98 Sqn
Canberra B2

WE113	WE122	WH670	WH911	WJ603	WJ611	WJ620	WJ635	WJ722	WK144
WK144	WK162								

Canberra T4   WD944   WT488
Canberra E15   WH948(8) WH957(7) WH954(4) WH972(2) WH973   WH981(1) WH983(3) WJ756(6)

115 Sqn
Varisty T1
WF383(E) WJ911(X) WJ946(M) WL622(R) WL636(D) WL678(C) WL685(S) WL692(P)
Argosy C1   XN815   XP412
Argosy E1
XN814 no name allocated   XN816 named "Iris IV"later"Phoenix"   XN855 named "Heleus"
XP413 no name allocated   XP439 named "Iris IV" later "Theseus"   XP448 named "Iris IV" later "Castor"
XP449 no name allocated   XR137 named "Orpheus"   XR140 named "Jason"
XR143 named "Omega"

Trials Flight
Argosy C1   XP450

231 OCU
Canberra B2
WL907(L) WH914(U) WH919(V) WJ637(Z) WJ674(Y) WJ677(X) WJ681   WJ728(J) WJ731(W)
Canberra T4
WE188(T) WE192(A) WE193   WH843   WH848(E) WJ861   WJ869   WJ870(F) WJ877(V) WT480(B)
WT482(C) WT483(D) WT488

360 Sqn
Canberra T4   WD944   WJ862   WJ863(U&Z)   WT488(Y)
Canberra T17
WD955(Q) WF890(M) WF916(P) WH646(G) WH664(H) WH665(J) WH740(K) WH863(L) WH872(W) WH874
WH902(N) WJ565(C) WJ576   WJ581   WJ607   WJ625(D) WJ630(E) WJ633(F) WJ977(R) WJ981(S)
WJ986(T) WK102(A) WK111(B)

Tri-national Tornado Training Establisment
Tornado GR1

ZA319 (B11)	ZA320 (B01)	ZA321 (B58)	ZA322 (B50)	ZA323 (B14)	ZA324 (B02)	ZA325 (B03)	ZA327 (B51)
ZA329 (B52)	ZA330 (B08)	ZA352 (B04)	ZA353 (B53)	ZA355 (B54)	ZA356 (B07)	ZA357 (B05)	ZA358 (B06)
ZA359 (B55)	ZA360 (B56)	ZA361 (B57)	ZA362 (B09)	ZA369 (BR61)	ZA373 (BR60)	ZA405 (BR62)	ZA540 (B12)
ZA543 (B59)	ZA548 (B10)	ZA652 (B15)	ZA599 (B16)	ZA602 (B13)			

4301 (G20)	4302 (G21	4303 (G22)	4304 (G23)	4305 (G24)	4306 (G25)	4307 (G26)	4308 (G27)
4309 (G28)	4310 (G29)	4311 (G30)	4312 (G70)	4313 (G71)	4314 (G72)	4315 (G31)	4316 (G32)
4317 (G33)	4318 (G77)	4319 (G78)	4320 (G73)	4323 (G34)	4324 (G74)	4325 (G75)	4326 (G76)
4329 (G35)	4331 (G36)	4335 (G38)	4337 (G37)				

55000 (I42)	55001 (I40)	55002 (I41)	55003 (I43)	55004 (I44)	7002 (I92)	7003 (I93)	7004 (I90)
7005 (I91)	7007 (I94)						

EVOLVEMENT OF AN AIRFIELD

The evolvement of the airfield involved many stages. From its origins as as a rolled, grassed area with just a few buildings, the station developed into a highly complex area of hangars, vast areas of concrete, support buildings and a small township of personnel accomodation. Many individual details of the stations development can be gained by studying the photographs in the main text, but nevertheless, it is impossible to list every stage of the stations evolvement, but luckily there exists a series of air-to-ground vertical photographs and maps that ably demonstrates this process.

The early days - Royal Air Force Station Cottesmore taken sometime during 1938
(Photo: Gp Capt W A Griffiths)

About ten years separates these photographs. *Above:* A poor quality mosaic with an overlaid grid of Cottesmore taken during the war, before the main runways were laid. Note the concrete perimeter track and numerous dispersal areas for aircraft. *Below:* The station during 1953 showing the three runways, including the extended 05/23 main runway for jet operations. *(Photos: MoD)*

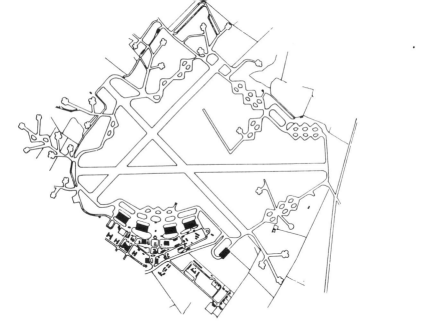

Two maps, thirty years apart. Above; The station as it was during 1950. Below: To meet the challenges of the next century the airfield has changed almost out of all recognition. Runway 05/23 has been extended even further, one of the cross-runways has all but disappeared, more dispersals have been built and a huge Aircraft Servicing Pan dominates the ground.

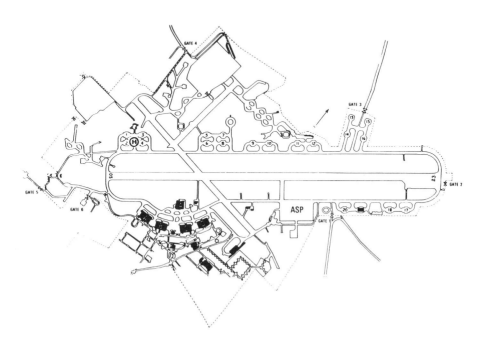

Acknowledgements

In writing this history I am particularly indebted to the Squadron writers of the Operations Record Books; the forms 540. These were the first and most important documents I consulted following an invitation from Air Cdre Probert of the Historical Branch, Ministry of Defence to use the facilities of his department. His staff were kind, considerate and went to endless trouble in producing the wartime records. The Operation Record Books tend to be fairly laconic documents written by busy Officers as a secondary duty and for background material, anecdotes and colour I consulted the following books:

The Right of the Line	John Terraine	- Hodder and Stoughton
Air War over France 1939-40	Robert Jackson	- Ian Allan Ltd.
Enemy Coast Ahead	Guy Gibson	- Michael Joseph Ltd.
The Golden Eagles	Peter Firkins	- St George Books of Perth.
Bomber Command	Max Hastings	- Pan Books.
The Bomber's Eye	Dudley Saward	- Cassell
The Mighty Continent	John Terraine	- BBC 1974
The Bomber Command War Diaries	Middlebrook and Everitt	- Viking.
The World at War	Mark Arnold-Forster	- Thomas Methren
Aircraft of the Royal Air Force since 1918	Owen Thetford	- Putnam
The Strategic Air Offensive Against Germany 1939-45. Official History	Webster and Franklin	- HMSO 1961
Not Much of an Engineer	Stanley Hooker	
Wings of War	Edited by Laddie Lucas	- Grafton Books
The Dam Busters	Paul Brickhill	- Pan Books
Action Stations 2	Bruce Barrymore Halpenny	- Patrick Stephens Ltd
Aeromilitaria 1/81		-Air-Britain
Wings Over Rutland	John Rennison	- Spiegl Press

In addition John Ellingworth, an enthusiastic aircraft researcher supplied me with information from his archives. I gleaned many other facts from conversations with local people including the widows of Squadron Leader Anderson, (one of the first Squadron Commanders) and Flying Officer Stanley Carter. Mrs Hester Brown provided me with documents concerning the early days of TTTE, Fred Mills, the Officers' Mess gardener supplied stories about post war activities at Cottesmore. I am honoured that Air Chief Marshal Sir Neil Wheeler not only should have written the foreword to this book but took the trouble to visit Cottesmore to talk about his early experience on 207 Squadron and allowed me to use his photographs of Fairey Battles. The book would not have been produced at all without the enthusiastic support of Group Captain Elder, Cottesmore Station Commander, who somehow managed to conjure funds to have it published. Flight Lieutenant Norman Roberson, who had already written the histories of XV and 20 Squadron, provided the dedicated attention to detail in endless correspondence all over the world to check details and collect additional authentic photographs. He sent the document to various authorities for criticism amongst whom Mr Roy Bonser was extremely helpful and gave us the benefit of his experience as an aviation writer. Norman provided the drive to see the project through to the end when I was leaving the Service and concentrating on preparations for a new job. Finally, despite being posted to the Gulf as part of Operation 'Granby' he managed to maintain almost daily contact with the publishers during the vitally important proof stage. It was a joint decision that any profits from the book should be donated to the RAF Benevolent Fund. I should like to thank Mrs Jackie Cole for typing innumerable drafts with unfailing good humour before we were satisfied.

The following have also been of great service: Lee Arbon, F W S Keighley R V Ashman, MoD - Air Historical Branch, D Benfield, Col R E Pace, T Convey, A Pearcy, Chaz Bowyer, J E W Price DFC AFM, Gp Capt G H Burleigh AFC, Public Record Office, G Cruikshank, RAF Museum, "Aeroplane",Wg Cdr E E Reeves MBE, W Ferguson, Maj L E Ross, R J Gosnell, Sqn Ldr C P Russell-Smith, B Goulding, Jack E Smith, P H T Green, Smithsonian Institution, Ground Photo Section - RAF Cottesmore, Wg Cdr E Stephenson, Grp Capt W. A. Griffiths, J. Dobson, R C Sturtivant, James J Halley, Flt Lt A S Thomas, G Hallion, USAFHRC - Maxwell AFB,Imperial War Museum, E Watts, Paul A Jackson and Cpl (now RAF retd.) Simon Ellis for the night photograph of the Tornado on the rear cover.

Finally I acknowledge the support given me by my wife Judy when so many weekends were taken up with research and writing when I might have been giving her the attention she deserves.

Jack G Talliss
Tickencote
May 1991